Outstanding Teaching, Outstanding Learning, Outstanding Leaders

by

Geoff Hannan

**Grosvenor House
Publishing Limited**

Geoff Hannan is hereby identified as author of this
work in accordance with Section 77 of the Copyright, Designs
and Patents Act 1988

The book cover picture is copyright to Geoff Hannan
Illustrations by Emma Bristow

This book is published by
Grosvenor House Publishing Ltd
28-30 High Street, Guildford, Surrey, GU1 3EL.
www.grosvenorhousepublishing.co.uk

A CIP record for this book
is available from the British Library

ISBN 978-1-908596-71-0

For the invisible children and those who see them

Student feedback

"This way of working is a lot better that the teacher babbling on!"

"It really gets your brain working."

"Made my think more, plan more and work harder."

"Class friendship has grown."

"We know each other better now."

"I like working with people I haven't worked with before."

"I think I work harder and better."

"Templates are good you can drop all the waffle."

"It's good to have time limits because you get on and don't muck around."

"Everyone gets an equal amount of say."

From Doncaster LA Improving Performance Project lead by Geoff Hannan

Contents

Reproducible Resources

If you would like an electronic version of this book on MS Word, PDF or any other format and a full copyright and network licence to reproduce the materials within your school then please contact Geoff Hannan direct on geoff.hannan@btinternet.com

Geoff Hannan and Angela Hannan Training and Consultancy International Chartwell, Sarn, Powys, SY16 4EY Phone 01686 670138

Preface

For over thirty-five years now I have been developing approaches and strategies for improving the quality of teaching and learning. Following my training sessions I am often asked by teachers and parents if I have a book with everything in it. I have written a number of books but, until now, none distilling what I would with hindsight consider the most important understandings and strategies. So here goes!

I hope it gives you many ideas and resources to use in your very important work.

I start where I am best known: with my work in gender differences. This has been the laboratory for many of my strategies...

CHAPTER ONE Gender Differences

Stereotyping is the blanket prescription of common traits to an entire group of people. Whilst categorisation is important to our understanding of the world and of one-another, stereotyping reduces uniqueness to its lowest common denominator. There are far many more differences *within* groups of people than there are *between* groups.

Good Equality and Diversity practice, on the other hand, is about valuing difference. It is about seeking to satisfy the differing needs that individuals and groups of individuals are *likely* to share because of their gender, ethnicity, social circumstance, abilities or disabilities. If we wish truly to value difference and seek to overcome the potential disadvantages that groups are likely to suffer, then we need to acknowledge these likely differences.

In what follows I provide a profile of the *average* boy compared to the *average* girl. The profiles are designed as tools to fine-tune our thinking to the needs of an individual student. I am not saying that ALL girls are like this and ALL boys are like that. I *am* saying that boys are likely to differ from girls in the following ways and for the following reasons. The categorisations may then become practical tools we may use as starting points to diagnose the needs of an individual child irrespective of their gender. Here goes!

Doers versus thinkers?

The average boy tends to be a "doer" first and a thinker, hopefully, second! The average girl is a thinker first and doer, hopefully, second. In the broadest of terms, good Equality practice in the classroom is about getting the girls into the doing and the boys into the thinking!

The typical boy has a much shorter concentration span that the typical girl. He is much more easily bored and more likely to be disruptive when he is bored. His verbal and literacy skills are weaker than hers. So too are his social skills and collaborative competencies. His listening skills are poor compared to her. He is less able to think reflectively, to plan and organise his work and follow linear processes from start through to end with adequate attention to detail. She, however, tends to be overly cautious and delivers too much detail.

He is differently and highly influenced by his peer group. He is likely to over-estimate his ability, she to underestimate it. She works harder and does more homework. She balances her school work with her social life: with him it's either one or the other. She is multitasking and can handle several operations simultaneously; he has to do one thing at a time. However, her confidence is lower and she is risk-averse in her behaviour.

Whilst she seems to be able to defer gratification, he seeks short-term, immediate reward and attention.

Her interest spectrum is centred upon relationships and people; his upon objects, systems and facts. He is more of a speculative thinker and a trial-and-error, experiential learner. She is more of a reflective thinker and a step-by-step, sequential learner.

Whilst the girl is in many ways a natural student, he is a boy first and the student, frequently, a poor second. She brings the chalk to the classroom, he brings the cheese!

I remind the reader that I am not seeking to present a stereotype, merely to present a list of potential learning disadvantages. No individual girl or boy will totally fit the above profile (although some come close!) Outstanding Teaching is gender- aware teaching and seeks to satisfy the needs of both males and females. Outstanding Learning is about developing and using both reflective and speculative skills. It is about being experiential and post-analytical as well as appropriately step-by-step. These are the bare bones of understandings onto which I put the meat of this book's strategies.

But enough now of the food analogies and into a brief synopsis of probable reasons behind boys' likely underattainment at school! If we get our teaching right for the group of children most likely to under- attain then we are likely to improve the learning of most students. The potential disadvantages that boys face in their learning mirror those of most lower attaining students irrespective of gender. So, onto the information that every teacher and every parent really ought to know about probable gender differences: if for no other or finer reason than it might just help us to be a little more tolerant of one-another...

Nature and nurture

We are what we are because of a complex interaction between "hard-wired" genetic influences and environmental factors. Let's not get into the chicken and egg debate here.

Suffice it to say that what came first is rather irrelevant to the chicken!

Although neuroscience is still in its infancy, there appears now to be a common understanding that the brains of women and men differ to some considerable degree. All human foetuses begin in the womb as female. Eight weeks or so into pregnancy, if the baby is to be a boy, testosterone bathes the womb and the foetus begins its "struggle to be male." As part of this process, it seems, male brains begin to develop differently. Women have more specialised language centres in their brain and men more specialised visuo-spatial centres. The corpus callosum which links the right and left hemispheres of the brain appears larger in women than in men (with the probable exception of some gay men and some lesbian women.) This may well afford the female easier cross-operation between the left and right sides of the brain. Emotional centres being largely situated on the right side and language centres on the left, the woman, it seems, may quite literally be more in contact with her feelings.

On average, boys are born larger and develop language more slowly than girls. With more focused eye contact, at six weeks, the girl will respond to a human face with a smile. The boy, whether it's a human face or a balloon! At six years, put two girls who are strangers to one-another in a room with some toys and by the end of half an hour they will know all about one-another and will be playing together. Two boys won't even know one-another's names and are likely to be playing separately. That's if they haven't had a fight in the meantime!

Let's give nature some credit in gender difference. Boys and girls are undoubtedly born with some differing genetic propensities. Propensities, however, are not destinies. Although, as a man, something in the genes helps make me what I am! I am a few million years up the evolutionary scale from my tree-swinging, nose-breathing forebears (despite my tendency to revert to type when my football team scores a goal or anyone remotely female crosses my field of vision!). I might be an emotional dyslexic but I can learn to train my animal instincts. Naked ape that I am, I am also a thinking one. Nurture too has its part to play.

The dolly and the car

Consider the differences in learning skills development as girls and boys come out to play. Typically the girl plays with her doll and the boy with his toy car. The girl is talking to her dolly. The boy is just making noises. Her early play activity is centred on relationships with people and his on relationships with objects. He may have a rich imaginative

landscape in his mind as he dashes around doing things but unlike her he doesn't verbalise it.

Not only does her play enrich and develop her language skills but also, early on, she begins to sequence her activities and follow linear processes. She will make up stories. Her stories will have a clear beginning, a progression and an end. He starts playing at or with something, stops and plays with something else. Now consider how much in learning is sequential, how much is about following linear progressions and how much is about seeing things through from start to end. Consider too the traditional stereotypical influences that affect the girl. She is more likely to help with the housework, go shopping and look after younger brothers and sisters. She is learning to take responsibility for herself and others in extended time frames. She is entrusted with tasks that develop her maturity. She learns to be attentive, neat and cautious. With probably genetic propensities in this direction, she learns to be caring and responsible. By Year-1 she has already developed many learning advantages over her male classmate. She can even sit at a desk without fidgeting!

This is not to say that the average boy isn't developing skills in other areas. He certainly is. He's a great explorer, more inclined to venture into new domains and seek wild and new experiences. On his trusty steed, with mighty sword in hand, he sallies forth to extend the reaches of his confidence; to heroically and single-handedly slay the dragons of his fears.

Playtime finishes with girls and boys sharing many similarities but also with some differences. In terms of learning skills the boys come in with more bruises!

I pause to say a fast word to the parents amongst you. To develop your small son's language skills it is likely to be of little use giving him a doll to play with. It is little use adapting girls' toys for boys. It is not "my little pony goes to the abattoir!" To develop his language skills, sit down with him as he plays with his car and get him to make up stories with it. Get him to verbalise more. And dads... you be the one that reads to him! You are an important role model to your young son. Don't let him grow up to think that it is just the women that read and talk about feelings.

Many parents will buy their daughters constructional toys and then discover that she prefers playing with her dolls. Indeed, a girl is only likely to play with Lego if she can make a little house with it, put a little person in the house and then make up a story. So sit down with her and get her to experiment more and take more risks in her play. Rough and tumble play is good for her too as it helps to develop her confidence. Mums... do non-stereotypical things with your daughters!

Dinner party man

Listen to people talking in, say, a pub or a restaurant and you will hear a sequence of communication emerge. The conversation will progress through stages that go Descriptive-Reflective-Speculative in that order!

Indeed, if you study any scenario where people are communicating well with others you are likely to find this progression. From simple sentence exchanges between neighbours in the street to complex interactions like a dinner party, this hierarchy is there.

Consider "Nice day isn't it?" "Better than yesterday!" "I wonder if it will last?"...even here, the sequence is Descriptive-Reflective-Speculative!

Now observe a typical dinner party. Conversations are heavily descriptive to begin with. People describe how they got there! They then proceed to describe recent activities in the past, for example, the holiday they have just been on. This takes the form at first of a blow-by-blow account of what they *did* on holiday: it's descriptive. Then it becomes reflective as feelings are attached to the actions previously described. People now go on to discuss what they liked or disliked about the holiday. Finally, when everyone is relaxed or drunk or both the conversation becomes Speculative. Deep philosophical conversations occur always at the end of the dinner party!

The descriptive-reflective-speculative progression is prevalent in many (if not all!) spheres of communication and learning. Consider how one uses it in counselling, mentoring and coaching. Consider its importance in the context of assessment and examinations: the B-Tec describe-analyse-evaluate demarcations for pass-merit-distinction being just one important example.

Use D-R-S in your teaching

A good lesson will follow the descriptive-reflective-speculative hierarchy. When things go wrong in the classroom it is frequently because these steps are missing or out of sequence.

I saw a lesson on Drugs Education where the teacher's starting point was "what can we do about the problems of drugs?" Her start was speculative, communication was strained and the children's behaviour quickly deteriorated.

This lesson should have been as follows. Stage One (Descriptive): *"You have five minutes, with the person next to you write down ten things you would think of as being drugs".* Stage Two (Reflective): *"Draw a line down your page. Select one of your drugs and see if you can find five good things and five bad things about it."* Stage Three (Speculative): *"Now select one of your bad things and let's discuss what we might do about it!*

Descriptive-Reflective-Speculative is how we communicate. It is also how we think and learn!

However, men and women tend to use the hierarchy differently!

I remind the reader that I am referring to the average woman compared to the average man. Not all women and not all men...

From simple to complex interactions, gender differences in this hierarchy as easy to hear.
Woman: *Nice day isn't it? Better than yesterday!* (Descriptive-Reflective)
Man: *Nice day isn't it? I wonder if it will last!* (Descriptive-Speculative).

Now revisit the dinner party and note the gender differences. We find that when the conversation is descriptive men and women are contributing fairly equally to the discussion. Although also note that the woman is likely to fill in the reflective details her partner misses out!

Midway through the dinner party as the conversation becomes reflective, the women are doing most of the talking. Finally when it gets heavy and deep at the end of the party the men take over, and the women might well be sitting back embarrassed by their partners!

The dinner party illustrates many gender traits, observe them! The man is a speculative thinker and communicator. He presents an argument and then post justifies it. He polarises. Something is either right or wrong. And he, of course, has to be right! He is confrontational: "I am right and you are wrong!" The woman is largely a reflective thinker and communicator. She communicates and thinks in the grey holistic area between the extremes of right and wrong. He has the mindset "I think" and speaks largely to communicate information and fact. She has the mindset "I feel" and speaks to communicate her feelings. Her approach is conciliatory rather than confrontational and she is much more likely to explore the whole issue. Finally her ease in communication itself allows her to think whilst talking. He works out what he is going to say and then says it! Men and women tend to communicate differently. Men and women tend to *think* differently.

DIY man

You can obtain some major insights into especially boys' under- attainment through a little observation of their adult counterparts. The boys' poorer reflective skills present a major weakness in their learning. Their weaker linear process skills perhaps an even bigger one! Consider self-assembly furniture and the differing gender approaches to it.

When putting something together, a woman more likely goes to the instructions first and follows them step-by-step. A man goes straight to the pieces and starts to assemble them. He *does* first whilst she organises, plans and *thinks* first. Let's develop the scenario a little further...

He often gets to do the job or takes over the job! After all, it's homemaking, its hunter-gatherer stuff is this... it's working with objects and he's expected to be good at it! He is a speculative thinker too whose male identity is rooted in his ability to solve problems. Why read the instructions? Any problems that emerge he'll be able to deal with as they occur, no sweat! But, of course, as a man he tends to overestimate his ability! He soon discovers that his skill levels do not support his confidence. Reluctantly he picks up the instructions. Luckily they are in the form of diagrams. Let's face it: he wouldn't bother to read them if they were in words. But now he is beginning to get frustrated and reverts to the level of a five year old child. At five when a child bumps into something it is always the something's fault. "Naughty chair!" the five year-old cries. "Bloody furniture!" yells DIY man. No, no, it's not his skill level that is the problem, it's the object he's working with!

Now, men are either brilliant or awful but seldom mediocre. Whilst you women can frequently luxuriate in mediocrity! You could be brilliant but your low risk-taking skills and low confidence inhibit you. Like a girl at school you do too much work: you go over and over the same things to make yourself feel totally secure and safe before you cautiously move on. Like a little boy at school, DIY man now goes one of two ways.

Ineffectual DIY man or boy at school gives up. He will now get easily diverted from the task in hand to something more immediately gratifying. This is possibly why men collect things more than women do! He has a row with his woman. Unable to deal with the emotional difficulties of the moment he picks up a newspaper and weeps in a general way for mankind instead! Or he goes to his den and fiddles with his stamp collection. Thus bad DIY man gives up and like a Year-11 boy with his homework will need to be nagged back into doing it.

At his best, however, DIY man, when faced with a problem will stay with it until it's solved. Take the computer as an example here. This highlights his experiential learning strengths. A new computer programme is learnt experientially. You download and play with it. The woman's linear learning style means that she more often than not would prefer to follow a manual step by step. Here, she is the one at a disadvantage for these days there is no manual. If he has a problem with his new programme he'll be up all night to solve it. If she finds difficulty she'll stop and get someone to tell her how to do it.

Either way, and eventually, DIY man completes the task. Now remember the boy's need for immediate gratification?

The first thing DIY man will now do is to call his wife in and show her the furniture. And, please note, now she dare not criticise! And what's the first thing she is likely to do with her great attention to detail? Well, find something wrong with it, of course!

When Dinner Party Man meets DIY Man

It would be remiss of me at this point not to mention how these simple observations are useful to us all.

When a woman has a problem she wants her partner to sit down and listen to her talk through this problem. Talking through the problem helps her to solve her problem, herself. She does not want or need yet frequently gets DIY Man. Rather than simply and actively listen to her, he is likely to sit there making suggestions. For all the best reasons he is doing the wrong thing. She then turns to him and says "You don't listen to me!" And she is absolutely correct. Men, you need to give your female partner or daughter or colleague time to let her talk through things. Ask questions, don't try to problem-solve for her! Avoid telling the female what to do!

DIY Man however is more likely to be a solitary problem solver. When he's got a problem he wants to go away and crack it on his own. He does not talk through his feelings; he works them out himself or disperses them through doing things. Dinner Party Woman may feel rejected on these occasions and that he doesn't need her support. Women, give him space! He is just different, that's all it is!

If you have an adolescent son then avoid nagging him! You know it doesn't do the slightest bit of good. Give him the knowledge that you are always available if he does wish to talk things through. Try to be non-judgmental. To get him to talk to you, *do* something with him. He is more likely to open up at half-time watching a football match.

Put nature/nurture and your sons and your daughters together with DIY and Dinner Party Man and what do you get? Subject outcomes at school!

MORE BOY-FRIENDLY SUBJECTS	MORE GIRL-FRIENDLY SUBJECTS
Maths	English
Physics	Modern Languages
Physical Education	Religious Education
	PSE
	Music
	Art
	Drama
	Integrated Humanities
	Biology
	Chemistry
	(History)
	(Geography)
	(Technology)
OBJECTS AND/OR SYSTEMS BASED	PEOPLE BASED
SPECULATIVE	REFLECTIVE
LEARNING MORE EXPERIENTIAL	LEARNING MORE LINEAR
DOING BASED	LANGUAGE BASED

The National Curriculum

A prime understanding for the provision and delivery of gender equality is that BOYS AND GIRLS ARE LIKELY TO HAVE DIFFERING LEARNING STYLES.

Rightly or wrongly the UK's National Curricula are much more girl-friendly than boy-friendly. This "feminisation" is easy to see in the changed outcome patterns in subjects such as technology and history (in brackets, above, for this reason.) Technology is boy-friendly when it is about doing and making things. The pre-and post-realisation emphasis of the National Curriculum places it now firmly in the girl-friendly reflective and analytical arena. Boys hold on well to factual information and like working with it. A history curriculum centred in fact is boy-friendly, one on evidence seeking and analysis is girl-friendly.

Only in Maths and Physics are the boys holding their own. These are strictly logical subjects. You are either right or wrong. There is no grey area in which the girls can thrive.

Don't despair, Lads!

Whether or not you agree in part or in whole with my theory of gender differences there are things you can do in the classroom to improve the performance of boys. You will find that the strategies in this book, whilst developed from the understandings above are not dependent upon them. They are good educational strategies irrespective of gender. We should be seeking to diminish the gender gap not obliterate it. Given the above, then girls should do better than the boys. Where schools have no gender gap or where the boys are out-performing the girls then we must challenge their practice. Girls and especially Working Class Girls are still under-performing in many areas. The strategies in this book will improve the performance of girls as well as boys, but not by as much. Thus they endeavour to narrow the gap and not to close it.

Strategies for Outstanding Teaching (1)

Gender Awareness

LIKELY GENDER DIFFERENCES
AND LEARNING NEEDS

MALE STRENGTHS
Confidence Risk-taking Speculative thinking Experiential/ Kinaesthetic Learning
Visual Learning Creativity

WEAKNESSES
Communication skills Literacy Linear skills Reflective thinking Attention span
Attention to detail Interpersonal skills Motivation Mono-tasking Externalises problems

STRATEGIES
- Good balance of experiential learning
- Add language to doing
- Short-term rewards
- Chunk Learning
- Break things down into 3-5 steps
- Write and read for purpose
- Use templates
- Encourage reflection and reflective explanation
- Teach collaborative skills
- Challenge
- Quicken pace

FEMALE STRENGTHS
Communication Skill Linear Skills Reflective Thinking Auditory Learning Likes writing Planning Organisation Interpersonal Skills Multi-tasking

WEAKNESSES
Risk-taking Speculative Thinking Low confidence Low expectations Internalises problems Takes everything personally

STRATEGIES

- Encourage risk-taking
- Encourage speculative thinking
- Reward effort and failure with effort
- Develop resilience
- Use communication skills especially in more boy-friendly subjects
- Communicate relevance
- Positive affirmation

Strategies for Outstanding Teaching (2)

Here are the likely gender differences and the interventions I would recommend to add to practice in early years settings. I have sectioned them under common Foundation Stage categories: +m= the probable male developmental advantage; +f= the probable female developmental advantage.

Personal, Social and Emotional Development

Perseverance- *Free selection +m Adult selection +f Concentration+f Attention Maintenance+m when motivated*

DIRECTED
- **BOY** Time and reward attention *Reward effort* Concentration games such as statues Copying games Sequencing games "Concentration Glasses" Copying pictures "Snap shots" (freeze techniques) Led gentle touching and stroking
- **GIRL** Create complicated tasks such as taking old computers/ machines to bits

FREE FLOW
- **BOY** Specify outdoor and indoor play areas some of the time and praise maintaining activity there
- **GIRL** Building pictures- models out of sand etc.

Forming of Relationships- *Peers through action lead activity +m organisational lead +f Adults- through role model and doing+m- through talking+f*

DIRECTED
- **BOY** Trust Activities in pair/group progressions Pair shape-making Pair musical chairs Pair in story-making Speaking together/role pairs Co-operation rewards
- **GIRL** Body bridges/stepping stones Imaginary carrying

Communication, Language and Literacy
Attention to what others say +f Initiation of communication +f Conflict resolution through language +f Attentive listening +f Active responding +f

Use talk to create play +f especially story making- subject specific +f people Interest in text +f Reflective Skills development +f Interest in illustration +m Interest in shape/rotations +m speculative skills development +m

DIRECTED

- **BOY** Question and Answer Teacher in role and children inventing questions Listen-and-copy story making games Teacher positioning during reading so children can see text as teacher reads Individual letter projection on whiteboard for writing over Led computer programmes projection programmes **Facilitate mark-making**
- **GIRL** Guessing games "Imaginary Walks" with details already laid out for exploration and question

FREE FLOW

- **BOY** Video loops of children talking to camera /giving instructions to be followed One-at-a-time activities to develop taking turns (monitored for behaviour checks and rewards)... script interventions (A say this, B say that) "Answer-phone" and computer messages (response and record) Small enclosed and especially roofed areas with props (telephones etc) Word building areas (name, place, age) Write-and-stick walls Text projected on whiteboards for drawing over (start with child's name)
- **GIRL** Pattern play

Mathematical

Linear +f Symbolic +m emerging

DIRECTED

- **BOY** Round robins with spoken and held numbers Number shape creation with bodies, plus adding, pairing Story number books Story making in sequence with numbers
- **GIRL** Clock play, led Rhythm games, music-making Memory and counting games Mix and match odds and evens Counting challenges in Groups

FREE FLOW

- **BOY** Hop scotch Skipping games Stepping stones with changing sequences (facilitate through challenge) Copying projected numbers Number sheets for colouring and copying "Three in a box" Jumble and sort numbers Number building blocks
- **GIRL** ICT Number games Clock play

Knowledge and Understanding

Emerging gender preferences- +m activity, hunting, aggression +f relationships, home-making

DIRECTED

- **BOY** Treasure hunts Detective games Come up and point Geography and map-making activities Dressing up Time Lines Google Earth Real story time Themed role plays in pairs groups I SPY
- **GIRL** Human bridges, circles, triangles etc Sound sequences Making music

FREE FLOW

- **BOY** Toy cars, trains, trucks, etc but add story making and questioning Toy swords, wands, super hero...with teacher facilitation... slow-mo play- teach care and consideration etc
- **GIRL** Balancing activities Building activities encourage Goo play fire fighters etc

Physical Development

Space +m Hand to eye +m Co-ordination large muscle groups +m Manual skills, precision co-ordination +f Hearing high frequency +f Male eye= movement focus

DIRECTED

- **BOY** Blindfold challenges Listening for sounds Let's build together Being small, being big Patting
- **GIRL** throwing catching kicking

FREE FLOW

- **BOY** Cranes and picking up activities Holding and feeling areas Big pencils and pens Threading challenges
- **GIRL** Small ball play, bean bag netball Bowling and target games

Creative

Using objects representationally +m Verbal +f

DIRECTED

- **BOY** Big sheet painting Story telling using objects Making music using objects Words with junk Puppet shows
- **GIRL** Making puppets Making landscapes

FREE FLOW

- **BOY** Puppets
- **GIRL** Junk play Cardboard boxes Newspapers Rags Plastic bottles etc Painting junk Making costumes Rubbish music-making

General Points

- Monitor individual children's use of free flow activities and engagement in directed activities - differentiate for individual child to fill gaps in experiences and for early intervention
- Think gender for when you examine how you can enrich the play environment
- Encourage especially boys to talk and co-operate
- Reward talk as well as action from boys
- Get especially girls to build, create and do
- Especially with boys: when answering questions keep responses short and wait before asking follow-up questions. If not forthcoming then ask child a subsidiary question: praise response.
- Especially with girls: let the children take the lead. Don't do too much for them.
- Challenge especially girls to solve problems. Reward effort. Reward failure and continuing attempts to do things
- Be aware of and break unconscious gender typing e.g. asking boys to carry things and girls to help wash up.
- Use Plan Do Review consistently before and after activities

CHAPTER TWO Go For Five

Bet especially a boy that he can't do something and he'll pretty soon prove you wrong! Learning is an intellectually active process. **Communicate challenge** more and it will help to motivate children into activity.

Variety is a highly important key for all children in their learning. Boys especially so. Think "challenge" and with a small step of the imagination you can turn even the potentially dullest of curriculum areas into an adventure! Studying a book could become a five day detective game played in teams. Early foreign language learning could become a space journey to an alien planet where the brave astronauts are preparing themselves for mankind's first contact. The Key Stage Three science class could become a laboratory team seeking a new industrial process for using magnets. Maths can become code-breaking.

Communicating challenge at the start of a more traditional lesson will help to motivate the students. Tell the class that they are going to find today's lesson difficult... they'll be able to do it... but they are going to find it hard! And you are helping immediately to make it more "child friendly." Be a little sensitive to the girls' reaction however. Bet a girl she can't do it and she might well agree with you! Here is your opportunity to talk about the way that girls tend to under-estimate themselves and boys over-estimate their skill levels. Use it.

Another important ingredient, especially although not exclusively, for boys is "time." A good rule of thumb, is to go for short time sequences rather than long ones. It is better for students to work intensively for short periods of time than half-heartedly for longer periods during which they have plenty of opportunity for distraction or creeping lethargy. **Break extended work down into manageable smaller units.**

As part of your variety of process, sequentially extend times on task. Rather than teaching for half an hour and then the students working for half an hour it is frequently better to teach part one for five minutes- students work part one for five minutes; teach part two ten minutes- students work part two ten minutes and so on. **Make activities at the start of the lesson "quick-fire"** ones designed to engage and motivate and as the lesson proceeds progressively lengthen the time the children are working. This extends their concentration span by stages as the lesson progresses.

Always apply a time structure to your homework assignments. Students will be more likely to do them! Again, this is an especially useful strategy for boys. Girls tend to do their duty first and then have their fun. With boys it is reversed. Girls are much more likely to do their homework first thing in the evening. The boy goes to his computer game first and by the time he's finished there's no time or incentive for his homework! The more open-ended the homework in terms of how long it might take the less likely he is to do it. If you say that a particular piece of homework will take the class thirty minutes and at the end of thirty minutes you can stop if you wish to, boys are more likely to do it first. Boys tend to put things on the back burner if they think they might take a long time.

I wrote earlier about the male need for immediate gratification. This makes the **communication of purpose** especially important to boys. Of course, it is important for girls as well but they are more likely to engage in a task simply because it is requested of them. "Why am I doing this? What's in this lesson for me?" These are questions you should answer by clearly communicating the purpose of your classroom and homework activities.

Communicate relevance in "student speak" at the start of the lesson: "during today's lesson you will be learning this, this and this." Tell the class why it is relevant. Not because the curriculum demands it but how relevant it is to them and their learning! At the end of the lesson check and get the class to check that they have actually learnt this something. It is especially important to demand the class to show-off their learning to one-another as this helps them to consolidate it through explaining it. **Use more quizzes**. These are particularly useful in aiding male motivation. "Learn this for homework and tomorrow first thing we are going to have a quiz." Not a test. Test is teacher versus child: a quiz is child versus child and picks up on children's competitive natures. Have extra merit points for those who do well and have put in a lot of effort or even small prizes. Another useful idea is score cards. Key skills, facts and understandings from any subject can be laid out for filling in as a score card as the curriculum progresses: explain this, do this and you score x points. Add your points and you get extra merits. You might think about extending the score cards into revision booklets.

And one final point before we get on to a more specific strategy: go for **quality not quantity**. One sentence or paragraph well written with time and care taken over it is better in learning than several pages reluctantly scrawled. Remember that we learn nothing *by* writing. (More, lots more, about that later!) But first: try this...

Go For Five

This very simple and easily applied strategy helps students to sequence and structure their ideas and their learning. It works like this:

Let's say that you have a problem to solve. ***First think of five possible solutions to the problem*** *and then select one.* You now get a far stronger solution to your problem. Using the "male" speculative strength, followed by the "female" skill of reflective analysis allows you get quickly and deeply into possibilities and find an appropriate course of action.

*Now **find five steps** in taking the selected action.* You are now breaking the process down into manageable stages. If you use this procedure for action planning then you will be much more likely to achieve your goal. The enactment will have enough precision without being over complicated and too unwieldy to handle. Go back to the profiles of the typical boy and the typical girl and you might see straight away how useful it is. The boy is likely to under-prepare, finding just three steps. The girl is inclined to be over elaborate and develop seven or so steps! It extends the boy's planning and appropriately clarifies the girl's.

GOING FOR FIVE has many other uses as well! For example, in written work. **Use Go For Five with Descriptive-Reflective Sequencing**. A history class is writing an essay: "What were the effects of poverty on Victorian England?" Instruct them not to write anything yet. Tell them first to *find five possible effects that poverty might have had.* Before beginning their essay ask them to make five single word notes at the top of the page. Next, instruct the class to write a paragraph for each of their ideas in turn: a paragraph that goes Descriptive-Reflective. That is, states each individual idea and then explains it. You are now providing a scaffold for the students to order, sequence and express their ideas. Again, this strategy turns out to be especially (although not exclusively) useful for the boys. All children are being trained as well in a highly useful examination technique!

Now consider a science class that has just done an experiment.
Before writing up your experiment look for five steps in what you have just done. The class is now reviewing the experiment with enough (and not too much) detail to remember it and to learn from it.

Use Go Five in preparation and to aid focus. For example in Food Technology...
"Before I begin the demonstration put the numbers one to five down the page in your exercise book, leaving two lines between each."

Deliver the demonstration in five steps and at the end of each instruct the students to write a few words to remind them of what to do.

"Boys make sure to write enough so that you will remember what to do and in what order! Girls don't write too much... trust yourself to remember what to do!"

The Drama Lesson...

"You have five full minutes planning time. Sit down with your group and plan five things that are going to happen in your playlet. O.K. boys... one thing can be a slow- motion fight!! But you have got to show me three things that lead up to it and, after it, one consequence!

This is an especially useful way of getting a more planned and thoughtful approach in boys' drama.

In English...

"Let's see if we can find five words that describe the character of Macbeth."

"I am going to show five things to look for in analysing a poem."

In Modern Languages...

"Schreiben Sie, bitte, funf Worter fur..."

In Geography...

"As your partner reads the paragraph on Switzerland make notes under the following five headings: Terrain, Climate, People, Imports and Exports. You will then tell us what you have discovered about the country.

In Music...

"As you listen to the music I want you to try to find five words that might describe it. You will then be asked to explain why you chose the words you did."

Why Five?

Listen out for this magic number! There is something deeply significant about five in our thinking. We are advised to take more exercise. How often? <u>Five</u> half-hour sessions a week. We are advised to eat more fruit and vegetables. How much? You know it! <u>Five</u> portions of fruit or vegetables per day!

How many styles of writing are there in National Curriculum English? Well, <u>five</u>, of course! The government puts forward a new plan. How many points to it? More often than not it will be a <u>five-point</u> plan. From the five working days in the week to the Five Pillars of Islam this number, more than any other has significance to us. Our decimal system is based on the abacus system of five. It will be because we have five digits on the hand. It will be because that's how we learn to count and to order things when small. It will be because, it seems, our brains hold onto things best in odd rather than even numbers. Quite unconsciously you will break down information you want to recall into groups of threes and fives, rather than twos or fours, or sixes. Try to recall an eight digit number and you are likely to end up forgetting one because the circuitry of our brains seems wired into odd rather than even "bites." Seven seems to the maximum in short-term recall, five is optimum.

Whatever the reasons behind it, five is ubiquitous. A five paragraphed history essay is a strong essay and scores high marks. Just like a three point political plan is rather bland and a seven point plan, unmemorable, so why five? Because four is too few and six is too many.

Try this in the classroom and note the different responses from the boys and the girls. Use this activity to illustrate how finding five ideas helps to develop our thinking and finding five steps helps to develop our planning. As well as using GOING FOR FIVE, get the students to understand WHY they should go for five.

The desert island and the mirror

Tell the class they are about to be stranded on a desert island. Fortunately they are prepared for such everyday eventualities. They have a survival kit. In this survival kit is a mirror.

Step One: Challenge them to find five separate uses that a mirror might have to help their survival.

Step Two: Select one of the uses, for example: to signal to a passing ship.

Step Three: Challenge them to find five important steps in using the mirror to signal for help. There are five significant ones:

1. Go to high ground.
2. Flash the mirror.
3. Look for a response.
4. Use Morse code to relay a message for help.
5. Look again for a response that gives you instructions.

Notice how the boys are likely to miss out steps whilst the girls are too elaborate. Notice how the girls want to clean the mirror first! Notice, however, how much more thought they give to the situation compared to the boys. The typical man stands on the beach and flashes the mirror with no chance of it being seen and the typical woman works out elaborate plans for using the mirror, by which time the ship has gone!

Step Four: Challenge the class to select a different use of the mirror and work out the five steps themselves.

Step Five: Discuss how useful GOING FOR FIVE is and when they might use it to help their planning and analysis.

Look no hands!

I feel that there is too much reliance on hands going up in the classroom. When a teacher asks for hands to go up, it is only the more confident students who are involved. It is also bad gender practice for girls. The ratio for boys' to girls' hands up in the classroom is on average three to one in favour of the boys. If you don't believe me then count!

Added to this, many students, like adults, require thinking space prior to answering questions. Give them this space and you also build their confidence and develop their reflective skills. Try this, especially at the start of the lesson. **Structured on-task talk prior to answering questions.**

*"Here is my question... talk with the person next to you... you have just one minute to find me **five** answers to my question."*

After the minute, still don't allow hands to go up, instead choose as many children as you can to participate and take responses from them *quickly*. **Use affirmation and praise.**

Affirmation (repeating back the student's response): *"Using a melon!"*

Praise: *"A good idea!"*

You are now doing some important things! You are requiring all the students to actively participate right then and there at the start of the lesson. Their involvement is now far more likely to be sustained. You are demanding the class to be reflective, to think before doing. You are structuring on-task talk at the start of the lesson. This is an important strategy. **Structure on-task talk** especially at the start of the lesson and you get less off-task talk! A simple mental check list as you take responses can now ensure that girls and boys answer questions equally. The boys still get three times the attention in the average classroom. (If you don't believe this then get someone to count during your lessons.)

In using TALK WITH THE PERSON NEXT TO YOU you are demanding the girls to take risks in presenting their opinions and ideas whilst allowing an opportunity for less confident boys as well as girls to prepare their responses. You are affording opportunities for immediate verbal praise (thus gratification) which is especially useful to the motivation of boys. You are also giving yourself opportunities to quietly get children on-task as you wander around the class.

And importantly, this strategy allows you to start the lesson with the students' own understandings and gives you an opportunity to assess their understandings. Use this strategy at the start of your lessons periodically and the pace will be enlivened. TALK WITH THE PERSON NEXT TO YOU is a simple idea that values the child's view as the fundamental starting point for learning. Try it!

AND FINALLY

At the end of the lesson- **Talk with the person next you and devise a question to ask.**

"Talk with the person next to you and devise a really difficult question to ask me about what you have just learnt. See if we can get five good questions from the class!"
Don't allow hands to go up. Go around the class again. Now you are requiring students to review and evaluate their own

understandings and to define their gains in learning to themselves.

Put these strategies together and you are actively teaching students two fundamental learning skills: to present ideas and to ask questions.

Challenge... you have five minutes... to improve the quality of your students' learning can you think of five other ways you might use the above strategies!?

Strategies for Outstanding Teaching (3)

Task with *Immediate* Purpose

Objectives

To improve motivation

To develop communication skills

To develop collaborative working skills

After you have written this you will be reading it to your partner

After you've read this we will be having a quick quiz on it

After you have drawn this you will be explaining it

After you've done this sum you will be explaining the steps

After you've rehearsed it you will be performing it to the class

Use Challenge

Objectives

To improve motivation

To develop relevance

Communicate difficulty... you are going to find this difficult!

Use time as a challenge... "Bet you can't find me five ideas in two minutes!"

Use "Parallel Challenges"- detective games- playing journalists/TV reporters- creating role plays/ "Personalisation"- making poems, songs- devising Power Point presentations- making videos

Have more quizzes

Challenge to show off learning

Use Timing

Objectives

To improve motivation

To develop urgency

To develop time management skills

Classroom Tasks

Homework

"A ten second explanation of..."

"A two minute role play on..."

Use "Go for Five"

Objectives

To develop in-depth thinking

Enhance and develop speculative and reflective skills

To develop linear process and sequencing skills

To develop organisational skills

To aid recall of information and understandings

Think of *five* possible solutions to a problem and then select the best

Think of *five* reasons why something might have happened before deciding on the most probable

Try to find *five* reasons for something and *five* reasons against something before making a decision

Find *five* good things and *five* bad things

Find *five* unknown things prior to seeking information

Five steps for doing things

Five steps for post-analysis

Five points to a plan

Five things to write about and then use Descriptive-Reflective

Learning in chunks of Threes and Fives

Strategies for Outstanding Teaching (4)

Use Partner Talk for answering questions
and a no-hands-up approach

Objectives

To improve the "variety diet" in the classroom

To enhance and develop communication skills

To improve collaborative working skills

To improve involvement

EXPLAIN THE IMPORTANCE OF ANSWERING QUESTIONS TO THE CLASS

Through answering questions you are putting understandings into your own words. This will help you to remember things better.

Through answering questions you have to think things through and this will help you to clarify your thoughts and understandings.

Through answering questions I can assess how well you understand things and how I can help you to improve your learning.

One reason for answering questions might not have occurred to you: it is to build your confidence. In answering questions you are "Risk-taking". Risking getting things wrong, risking stating your own ideas and opinions and, equally importantly, risking speaking in front of everyone else are important ways you build your confidence in yourself.

EXPLAIN THE TECHNIQUE TO THE CLASS

Answering questions is so important that everyone needs to do it. So this is how I am going to work with you for much of the time- I am going to tell you my question. Sometimes I will write it up on the board. Sometimes I will write a key word or prompt on the board. I will then give you just thirty seconds to talk with the person next you or with a partner to prepare your answer. Other times I will give you thirty seconds of individual thinking time. When the time is up I will <u>not</u> allow hands to go up; instead I will go quickly around the class and ask you to make your replies. I will ensure that everyone gets equal practice at answering questions.

It is effective to divide questions off into three broad categories: descriptive, reflective and speculative. This enables progression along the learning hierarchy (step one- how to do something or what something is; step two- why we do what we do/why something is as it is; step three- if I know what something is and why it is as it is; how

REPRODUCIBLE PAGE

© Geoff Hannan

can I use this knowledge to connect to new information and new understandings). Ask each type of question in each lesson and you will ensure a range of responses. The categorisation may also help you to differentiate.

Explain to the class that you will ask HOW, WHY and IF questions.

When you use TALK WITH THE PERSON NEXT TO YOU it is important to use affirmation and praise.

Quickly repeat back the child's answer (affirmation technique: it shows you have listened to the answer carefully) and reward it immediately by *Good Effort, Nice Idea, Interesting, Yes that is important* etc.

Another idea is to get each child to tick a grid in their planner or in the back of their note book each time thy answer a question in this way. Once they have answered X number of questions they get a special merit certificate/ bonus merit points etc.

WHEN YOU ASK A QUESTION EXPLAIN CLEARLY WHAT YOU ARE LOOKING FOR IN THE ANSWER FOR EXAMPLE

Find me three/five answers to my question

Find me five things you remember from last lesson

Find me five words that describe X

That uses the word X (Key Word, scientific/technical term etc) and explains what it means

That uses five steps to explain how to X (step-by-step explanation of doing something)

That provides a detailed response that explains why you think as you do

That uses a statement followed by the word "because..."

That gives a detailed response that explains why X (conceptual understanding) happens/is as it is

That illustrates by comparison using connectives such as *in the same way/equally/similarly/ as well as*

That attempts to contrast one thing with another using words such as *however/but/on the one hand, on the other*

That tries to persuade using words such as *obviously/of course/ clearly/surely/certainly*

That gives an opinion using words such as *it would seem that/ maybe/perhaps/definitely*

Etc Strategy link: "Go for Five"

CHAPTER THREE Use Templates

Below are the "Templates" I have developed to aid the thinking, planning and organizational skills that students need in learning. Although the concept is multi-adaptable the ones below are subject specific to illustrate in detail how, and for what reasons, they may be effectively employed. They all work on the basis of structuring "on-task talk" ideally in pairs so I shall begin with the English Template to explain the premises.

WRITER'S NOTE SHEET

I want to show or explore...

_____

1. MY STORY STARTS LIKE THIS:
THE SCENE:
THE CHARACTERS:
THEIR FEELINGS/MOOD:

2. THEN THIS HAPPENS_____

_____

_____

3. THEN THIS HAPPENS_____

_____

_____

4. THEN THIS HAPPENS_____

_____

_____

5. MY STORY ENDS LIKE THIS:
THE SCENE:
THE CHARACTERS:
THEIR FEELINGS/MOOD:

some interesting words and phrases I am going to use...

HOW IT WORKS

You give each pair of students in the class a copy of the above Template and with their partner instruct them to invent and talk through a story, say for ten minutes (thus prescribing **time**.) On the template they are to make short notes to remind themselves of what they are going to write about. After the ten minutes they then write their stories together and you also tell them how long you will be giving for this task. Importantly, you tell them that after writing their stories they will be reading them to one-another (here you are prescribing **purpose** to the activity.)

Developmentally **oracy precedes literacy**. I have discovered that if a student talks through an activity prior to doing it then they will do it better. The Template, using "Going for Five," leads them through the important story making considerations sequentially and helps them to focus and structure their work.

In story making, boys seldom express feelings ("Big boys don't cry!). Good stories however rely on mood transition. If a character starts happy and ends sad, for example, this leads naturally to plot considerations: what happens to change things. This consideration thus requires the *reflective* analysis that boys especially need in order to improve their work. Simultaneously, it is helping the girl to simplify her over-elaborate analysis. During the ten minute planning phase, the girl is also demanded to go straight for content rather getting her tippex out!

The last box in the Template is about the "deconstructing of language" and I shall refer to this strategy in detail in a later chapter.

All the Templates are designed to be used as part of a variety of activities. Not all the time so that they become boring but consistently, every few weeks or so, to actively teach process skills.

I was interested to see when I first introduced this idea through my training many years ago how templates were quickly taken up and I still see them being used in many schools today. They were, I think, precursors to writing frames. These are very useful but the basic idea behind my templates is that they are "thinking frames" and designed to be used as part of a variety of processes to improve students' thinking and their linear progressions through task.

****

The Technology Template is designed for both planning and post analysis and I suggest below some other ways you might use *all* the Templates to enrich variety in the classroom...

TECHNOLOGIST'S
PROCESS SHEET

DATE:_____

TO:_____

_____

I WILL USE:

I WILL

STEP ONE:
_____

STEP TWO:
_____

STEP THREE:
_____

STEP FOUR:
_____

STEP FIVE:
_____

THIS WENT WELL:

1._____

2._____

3._____

THIS WENT NOT SO WELL! _____

_____

WHY?_____

NEXT TIME I SHOULD:_____

_____

The Technology Template might be used so that each of the boxes incorporates a full page to allow more detailed diagrams and bullet points. It is designed to provide a simple and universal tool to aid the pre-realisation and post-realisation stage. It is good to see how many technology departments have run with the idea and developed it. I visited one school where they had enlarged it to A2 and surrounded it by technological terms and expressions that the students could use in producing their folders.

As part of a varied "diet" *periodically* use the Technology Template as follows:

Prior to engaging in the technological task and after teacher demonstration (perhaps in three to five steps!), the students are each given the template below and allocated planning time to complete it...

"You have ten minutes. With your partner talk through the process you will use and in each box write down just a few notes or a diagram to remind yourself of the steps you will be taking and the order you will be taking them in. Make sure that you find five steps in your planning."

You should, of course, also debrief the *purpose* in using the template...

"This activity will help you put enough detail into your planning to successfully complete your design realisation."

Ensure that nobody commences the realisation until the ten minutes are up. Use the time as you move around the classroom, to extend the thinking of the high attainer and assist the lower attainer. The instruction "or a diagram" should help the latter in completing the pre-realisation phase on time.

When the time is up, make sure that all students now get into the making phase and set an appropriate time for this activity. Ensure that the girls, too, start making the product!

On completion of the realisation give the following instruction...

"You have X minutes to evaluate the process you have used by finding three things that you feel went especially well and writing these in the THIS WENT WELL boxes. Take care with your writing. Write your statements neatly and check the spelling of words you are not sure of. Use the correct Technological terminology. I shall write some of the words you might wish to use on the board. Write in short sentences and take care over your punctuation as well."

Explain the purpose...

"This will help you when you come to revise your work and when you answer examination questions. It is important to express your ideas accurately and concisely using the correct terms."

"Finally, when you have done this, in the THIS WENT NOT SO WELL box evaluate one thing you found especially difficult or something you were not so happy with in the task you've been through; and, importantly, target an improvement: by stating how you would do it differently next time to improve your performance."

Explain the purpose...

"This will help you to develop your evaluation and self-assessment skills and help to improve the way you do things next time."

VARYING THE USE OF THE TEMPLATES

The templates may be used effectively and periodically on an individual basis, and in pairs and in small groups using just one template.

You will also find the template system useful in helping the students to present their experiences to others in the class, thus further enriching core skills development work and helping to develop their confidence.

I am a great believer in the importance of **communicating reasons** *to students. Too often we ask students to do things without them understanding why.*

Example

"In your working groups and now that you have filled in your templates, I am going to ask you to take these sheets to another group and in turn make a report to them on how your group conducted the realisation and how you evaluated it. After you have made your report, it is "question time". The other group should try and find some really difficult questions to ask you. For example, you might like to ask them to explain why they did things in the order that they did them and not in another sequence. Through this activity you will be doing some important things in your learning. You are helping to develop clear communication skills. This is important not just in your school work but outside school as well. Communication skills are very important to develop good teamwork practices which are used a lot today in the workplace. You will also be justifying and defending your ideas which helps to build your confidence. You are also learning to constructively criticise others and to take constructive criticism yourself. It will also help you to remember what exactly it is that you have been learning!"

USE TEMPLATES TO DIFFERENTIATE

One group might be given, for example, an intricate task to develop their organisation and design skills.

"Now that you have decided what you are going to make and as a group filled in the template, to really challenge you to look in detail at the realisation process I am going to give

this group five more templates! The challenge is to break each of your initial steps down into five smaller ones!

Another group might be given a task to develop their teamwork skills.

"Now that you have completed your template allocate responsibilities within your group so that each team member is responsible for a different step in the making. Being in charge of this step will help to develop your team leadership skills."

A third group might be given a template to evaluate the work of other groups during the making.

"Your group will be a Quality Control Team during today's lesson. Whilst the other groups are planning you must plan your quality control process using the five steps."

Think about the potential of devising say three separate group work tasks which put together encompass all the learning objectives of a particular programme of study. When the groups present back and examine one-another's work they will be covering much of the curriculum in a shorter period of time! You should find the Template system very effective in this.

****

The Science Template is designed to be used after an experiment to encourage dialogue and analysis. It requires the students to look in enough but not too much detail at their experiment and to extract a simple and significant statement of learning. This should be written neatly, using correct scientific terminology. Short sentences help students remember information and short sentences in short paragraphs get good marks in science exams!

SCIENTIST'S ANALYSIS SHEET

DATE:_____

EXPERIMENT _____

_____

I DID

STEP ONE:

_____

STEP TWO:

_____

STEP THREE:

_____

STEP FOUR:

_____

STEP FIVE:

_____

I DISCOVERED:_____

_____

_____

I HAVE LEARNT:_____

_____

_____

The Modern Languages Template is designed as a tool for helping students to appreciate and use grammatical structures. A sentence is cut up into its constituent words and the task is, with your partner, to put the words in the correct order on the Template. Build up a resource bank of different key grammatical structures. One is done for you as an example.

GERMAN SPEAKERS CUT AND PASTE GRAMMAR GAME

WHO:

DOING:

WHEN:

HOW/WITH/IN WHAT MANNER:

WHERE:

ICH

DU

ER

SIE

WIR

SIE

SPIELE

SPIELST

SPIELT

SPIELT

SPIELEN

SPIELEN

UM ACHT UHR

MIT MEINER KATZE

MIT UNSERER KATZE

MIT MEINER FREUNDIN

MIT UNSEREN FREUNDINNEN

IM PARK

THE SPECULATION TEMPLATE

For any speculative process use a Speculation Template to teach the linear skill behind effective problem solving. Try to solve the problem below without assistance and then see how useful the Template system can be in helping you! Here goes...

John says "I didn't do it!"
Varindar says "He's lying!"
Cindy says "I am innocent!"
Two people are lying. Who did it?

SPECULATION SHEET

I WANT TO FIND OUT:_____

I THINK THAT:

I CAN TEST THIS BY:

RESULT:

I NOW THINK THAT:

I CAN TEST THIS BY:

RESULT:

I NOW THINK THAT:

I CAN TEST THIS BY:

RESULT:

I HAVE DISCOVERED THAT:

DEBRIEF (IF YOU NEED IT!)

I want to find out: *Who did it (not who is lying! You can't discover this until you find who did it!)*

I think that: *Yes, you have to "guess and test" to solve the problem.*

I can test this by: *Assume that John did it and see if it fits the facts that two are lying.*

Have a go with the Templates and <u>experiment</u>: make some more up yourself. Just remember the key ingredients: structured on-task talk within a set time and, of course, GOING FOR FIVE.

A few years ago I experimented with the template idea more deeply and discovered that by staging the lessons carefully and using Think-Communicate-Write through pair work you could substantially improve the quality of students' writing and their recall of content. I explain Think-Communicate-Write in more detail in Chapter Six and the learning Partner idea in the next chapter but here I enclose the lesson plans and templates. Please feel free to adapt and make your own. Many teachers have run with these ideas and finessed them to suit their individual subjects and circumstances.

Strategies for Outstanding Teaching (5)

Use Templates

As communication and thinking frames to teach students how to progress through tasks, especially and consistently prior to writing.

Use Writing Partners

Consistently use Learning Partners as Writing Partners so that students write together: one piece of work with one partner being the scribe. Change the scribe each time.

Use Think-Communicate-Write

Objectives
To develop communication skills
To develop writing skills
To develop reading and learning skills

Break approximately 50% of writing activities down into three stages:
- *Students think about and plan what they are going to write*
- *Students explain out loud to their partner before they write*
- *Students write*

Similarly, ask the students to use the three stages with their Writing Partner.

Request that students read out loud what they have written to their Learning Partners.

Writing Partner Resource 1
General Writing

How it works

A picture is copied and pasted into the box on the left of the page and key words/ phrases are added prior to printing.

The students are given just one sheet between them.

Time is allocated for each of the following activities in turn:

Learning Objectives

Teacher Introduction: 5 Minutes

Step 1: 5 Minutes

➢ Talking with your partner: ***describe*** the picture/scene/situation/ topic/content. Challenge: see if you can find five detailed descriptions of the picture/topic. These will explain what is happening/ what it is/ what are the steps in doing something/ how to do something. MAKE NOTES IN THE DESCRIPTIVE BOX.

Step 2: 5 Minutes

➢ Talking with your partner: ***reflect*** upon the picture: see if you can find three detailed reflections upon it. These will answer the question "why?" in some way or analyse it further: Why are the people doing what they are doing? Why does/did this happen? Why are things done in this order? Analyse the good and the bad things about it. Analyse the causes. Analyse the effects. MAKE NOTES IN THE REFLECTIVE BOX.

Mini Plenary: 5 Minutes

Step 3: 20 Minutes

➢ Working it out as you go with your partner (taking turns to write or writing individually in your own exercise book) create a detailed piece of writing **together**, sentence by sentence. Firstly, describe in detail. Secondly, analyse in detail. Use a combination of short and extended sentences. Use connectives.

Step 4: 5 Minutes

➢ When you have finished, take turns to read it out loud to one-another. Correct and improve it where necessary.

Step 5: 5 Minutes

➢ Taking turns with your partner, read your pieces to the class/ other Writing Partners.

Plenary: 5 Minutes

THINK-COMMUNICATE-WRITE   Name: _____

My Writing Partner today is _____

Subject: _____ Date: _____

Teacher/student...paste
your picture/diagram here:

WHAT

DESCRIPTIVE

1

2

3

4

5

WHY?

REFLECTIVE

1

2

3

Teacher/student...type or write your key words here:

OUR WRITING

D ————————————————————————
E ————————————————————————
S ————————————————————————
C ————————————————————————
R ————————————————————————
I ————————————————————————
P ————————————————————————
T ————————————————————————
I ————————————————————————
V ————————————————————————
E ————————————————————————

R ————————————————————————
E ————————————————————————
F ————————————————————————
L ————————————————————————
E ————————————————————————
C ————————————————————————
T ————————————————————————
I ————————————————————————
V ————————————————————————
E ————————————————————————
————————————————————————
————————————————————————
————————————————————————
————————————————————————
————————————————————————
————————————————————————
————————————————————————
————————————————————————
————————————————————————
————————————————————————
————————————————————————

Writing Partner Resource 2
Reflective Writing

This process can be used for any reflective writing activity:
- Creative story-making
- Studying plot lines in literature
- Studying cause and effect in History
- Studying, for example, physical processes in Geography
- Studying processes in Science
- Understanding how the body functions in PE

Group work in 4s by joining two Writing Partners

Learning Objectives
Teacher Introduction: 5 Minutes

Step 1: 5 Minutes
- ➢ Explain the idea of the tableau. Tell the class that they will be creating a series of tableaux exploring the subject content of the lesson. Explain that when they have created their tableaux they will then come out in their groups and create the scenes in order in front of the class.
- ➢ Brainstorm the kinds of scenes they might create/steps in doing something/main events in sequence etc.

Step 2: 10 Minutes
- ➢ Using stick men/line drawings (no colouring-in needed!) on Resource 3 the students plan out their tableaux sequence. Give out one sheet per group enlarged to A3

Step 3: 10 Minutes
- ➢ In turn the groups show their tableaux. As they are shown ask questions exploring *what* is happening and importantly *why* it is happening and *why* they chose to show things in the way they have.

Mini Plenary: 5 Minutes
Focus on the reflective content expressed by the students
Step 4: 10 Minutes
- ➢ In the previous groups the students now devise <u>detailed *descriptive/reflective*</u> statements about each tableau, writing these in the oval shapes.

Step 5: 15 Minutes
- ➢ The tableaux are re-shown and the statements are read out during each.

THINK-COMMUNICATE-WRITE   Name: _____

My Writing Partner/Group today is _____

Subject: _____Date: _____

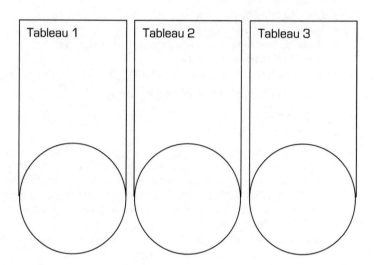

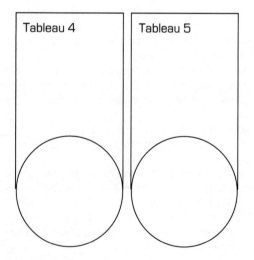

Writing Partner Resource 3
Template for in-depth
reflective thinking/writing

Learning Objectives
Teacher introduction: 5 Minutes

Step 1: 5 Minutes
  ➢

Step 2: 5 Minutes
  ➢

Step 3: 10 Minutes
  ➢

Mini interactive plenary: 5 Minutes

Step 4: 15 Minutes
  ➢

Step 5: 5 minutes
  ➢

Interactive plenary: 5 Minutes

THINK-COMMUNICATE-WRITE   Name: _____

Reflective Writing   My Writing Partner today is _____

Subject/Title: _____Date: _____

PICTURE   POINTS   ANALYSIS

Teacher/student
insert/draw your
picture here

Teacher/student
insert/draw your
picture here

Teacher/student
insert/draw your
picture here

Some ideas for partner talk

Preparation

A and B separately prepare ~they choose to be a person, place or process. They note down five details about their choice or five steps to the process.

In turn by asking questions they have to discover what their partner has chosen.

Interviewing

Preparation

A and B separately prepare ~they chose to be a person, place or process. They note down five details about their choice or five steps to the process.

In turn they interview one-another as if in a TV chat show in order to discover as much about the person, place, or process as possible.

Post Analysis

Following an activity together A and B note five important steps in doing the activity and then, together, write a short paragraph that explains exactly what has been learnt by the activity using correct subject-specific terminology and key words.

Listing

Alternately A and B list subject specific descriptions, terminology or key words. The challenge with your partner is to repeat the longest list (without notes to help) out loud after the given preparation time.

Sequence Building

In turn A and B have to build a detailed sequence for doing something.

A begins by saying "step one is to...." B then says "step two is to..." and so on.

The challenge with your partner is to repeat the longest sequence (without notes to help) out loud after the given preparation time.

Planning

Together A and B plan five steps prior to doing something together. They mime it afterwards (this helps recall).

Discussion

A prepares 5 good points or reasons for something.

B prepares 5 bad points or reasons against something.

In turn they debate each point.

Each must then select 2 of their partner's statements that are strong points well made.

Grids

Each pair is given a grid with, for example, columns "for" and "against". They are then given a list of information to place in the grid by agreement. Anything they can't decide upon is left for more detailed discussion at the end of the allotted time.

Selection

Each pair is given a list of words, subject specific terms etc. and have to select five most appropriate to their views or the content being worked on.

Some ideas for partner talk (2)

Questions
Pairs are given time to devise quiz questions to test the understandings of other pairs/class.
When questions are being answered the pairs work together to agree on their answers

Reviewing
Pairs together find five things they recall from the previous lesson.

Diagrams/Mind Maps
Pairs devise together, through discussion, one diagram or mind map re a specific topic

Questions 2
Pairs swap exercise books with one-another and are given time to devise questions to ask each other re specific topics.

Note taking
Prior to teacher reading or presenting information, pairs are briefed to individually make important notes or listen for key information. They then compare notes and select the five most important details.

Joint answers
Teacher asks a difficult question ~pairs are given a short period of time to find the correct solution together.

Descriptive development
After watching something pairs have to find as many words as possible to describe it. They then have to prioritise the most important descriptive details.

Paragraph construction

In Pairs they have to create an extended piece of writing that uses certain words, e.g. Firstly, Secondly, Thirdly, Next, Finally.

Presentations

Together the pairs are challenged to be teachers for one minute and prepare and present a talk to the rest of the class about a certain topic, aspect or curriculum content. Each pair in the class is given a different subject to work on.

Role prescriptions

A is given one role, for example to be descriptive, to be against something, to select nouns. B is given another role, for example to be reflective, to be for something, to select verbs. They relate their selections back to one another.

For calculations

Pairs do different mathematical calculations together and delineate steps to follow in future.

They then teach another pair to follow their steps.

Practical work

Following practice of a sequence of skills, pairs select a specific skill and break it down to describe to another pair. Together they speculate how to improve the skills.

Some ideas for partner talk (3)

For quick recall
Following teacher demo of skills/process to be carried out, pairs plan how they will work together and allocate roles to one-another.

Following ICT activities
Computers are turned off and pairs are challenged to explain the process step by step so as not to forget it next time.

Practical work 2
Pairs watch another pair perform a task. Following discussion they suggest improvements.

Read/Think/Communicate1
A reads out loud to B, B notes five important points or five steps etc. They then tell their partner what they have selected and prepare to present back.

Read/Think/Communicate2
A is challenged to find, read and note information about a topic, B about a related topic. After the allotted time they share information with their partner, find common factors and prepare to present them back.

Read/Think/Communicate3
An important question is given by the teacher. In pairs they speculate on possible answers prior to looking up the information.
They prepare their answer to present it back together.

CHAPTER THREE A third, a third, a third

STRUCTURING PAIR AND GROUP WORK

*The most significant improvements in performance I have seen in the many schools I have worked with have been through the introduction of **Learning Partners**...*

This is quite possibly *the* most important strategy you can apply for improving boys' performance. I recommend that, of your pair work, one third should be friendship pairing; one third in single-gender non-friendship pairings (for example, partners with similar learning styles preferences and mixed-ability learning partners); and one third in mixed-gender pairings and groupings. And this should take the form of a "rolling programme" of such work so that during the time-span of half a term, all pupils work in a *structured* way with every other pupil in the class.

What one mostly sees in schools is informal friendship pairings in the classroom. Children who are friends with one-another sit together and, although working individually, are allowed to communicate if they need to.

If you take one worksheet or book away and instruct them to work together on the task you are now into Proximal Learning and new opportunities for skills development open up...

Rationale

There are fundamentally two ways that children (and for that matter, adults as well) learn anything: individually and "proximally," i.e. together with another child. If you listen in on two children working together on a task you may readily appreciate the importance and the unique qualities of this type of learning. They are explaining things to one-another in appropriate language and discussing new concepts at their level of comprehension. In short, they are extending their conceptual understandings and learning skills on a child-centred level that the adult would find difficult, if not impossible, to communicate on. Consider learning something new and difficult yourself. Clearly you would need a good teacher. But also consider the added benefits of having another new learner working with you in unravelling, say, a new and difficult concept.

In the school classroom there are also many other benefits to this approach.

When two boys work together on a task inevitably one will take the lead and the other will follow, with little language interaction between them. Put that boy with a girl and you will find much more communication will take place. Analyse the quality of the communication and you will soon discover that the boy is now having to be REFLECTIVE and the girl SPECULATIVE, helping to compensate for likely gender disadvantage. The boy is having to defend his highly confident yet, quite probably, highly dubious speculations and reappraise them! The girl is demanded to be speculative: to extend beyond what to her are easier reflections into presenting and justifying alternative propositions. The upshot is that both are now enhancing and developing core language and learning skills. Simultaneously you are helping the boy to extend his social skills.

Apply the A THIRD, A THIRD, A THIRD pluralism to this process and you are giving all students in the class periodic and structured access to the high-order language and learning skills of the most gifted. This is a mutually enriching access. A high-attaining student in helping a low-attaining student is learning to simplify, express and explain their understandings. Ironically, one of the ways we actually learn most effectively is through teaching! In teaching someone else we have to structure and sequence our own understandings and express them in a form that is easily accessible. Consider the importance of this skill to examinations! Remember, however, A THIRD, A THIRD, A THIRD means that the most able are also working together to consolidate and extend their own high-level skills.

In applying THIRD-THIRD-THIRD you are also developing a classroom environment that is effective in developing girls' confidence. Structured access to working with boys will help to develop especially the girls' self-assertion skills and their ability to deal with male dominance and attention-seeking.

IMPROVING BEHAVIOUR
Rotation is the key!

In structuring group work in this way you are also facilitating good behaviour in the classroom. You will find that A THIRD, A THIRD, A THIRD works in two ways for producing an easier classroom to manage.

It breaks up the blocks of potentially troublesome friendship groups of boys which give teachers most irritation. For two-thirds of the group work time they are not physically together with their friends and are required to co-operative with other pupils in the class.

Importantly, as well, you are helping all students in your class to feel more confident and comfortable with one another. You will find after a while that there will be far fewer "put-downs" and that the students will be getting on much better with one another. A THIRD, A THIRD, A THIRD is a fundamental anti-bullying practice and for similar reasons a highly important antiracist and anti-sexist strategy.

Sadly two children may be in the same class with one another for five years without once ever working together. What practical use are our antiracist and diversity policies when, for example, Asian Origin and White students are never actively encouraged to work together? Neither will boys and girls work together unless we demand it. The class remains too often a group of strangers. You have the opportunity in your classroom to develop something far more important than learning your subject. ***You have the opportunity to develop tolerance and respect between the sexes and the races!***

One final point. The children who most need to develop their social experience and interpersonal skills in this way are the ones least likely to be given the opportunities. Group work is frequently perceived to be more trouble than it's worth with the more challenging "working class" child (and boy specifically!) One observes far more group work in schools with a "middle class" catchment. All children need access to these competencies. Here's how...

MANAGING THE DEVELOPMENT

You might like to begin to work in this way from scratch with a class that is new to you or with an older class that you have established a good relationship with. If you are a Secondary teacher not used to working in this way then you might like to use the strategy with just one of your Year-7 classes for one whole term to train yourself. Then you'll be able to adopt it with your other classes. Best of all is to have a Departmental Policy/Whole School Policy to support the practice.

Sit this class, initially, boy-girl around the room. Immediately you will find the classroom calmer and easier to manage. Then it is important to tell the class at the outset how and why you intend to use A THIRD, A THIRD, A THIRD. A good way of doing this is to display a poster and discuss it in detail with your class, proactively confronting their reservations. After all it's only their embarrassment!

OUR WAYS OF WORKING

DURING LESSONS YOU WILL BE WORKING
IN THE FOLLOWING WAYS FOR THE FOLLOWING REASONS:

1. INDIVIDUALLY
To develop your own individual learning skills and enjoyment of our subject

2. WITH LEARNING PARTNERS
To learn to help one-another and work co-operatively
To develop your communication skills and life skills
To learn "experientially"- to learn through doing things yourself <u>and</u> with others

3. YOU WILL HAVE THREE LEARNING PARTNERS
Girl-boy: so you help to develop both reflective and speculative approaches and learn to cooperate with people of the opposite sex.
Friendship: where you choose whom you want to work with and help one-another to learn.
Learning Styles partners: where you will be working with someone who prefers learning in a similar way- kinaesthetic, visual or auditory. We use *differing* communication skills with our friends and with others we are not as close to and working this way helps to develop better communication and learning skills as well as helps to build our confidence and teamwork skills with other people.
Working this way will help you develop your confidence and build new friendships.

SWAPPING

Begin applying A THIRD, A THIRD, A THIRD, by organising **three Learning Partners:** boy-girl, single-gender friendship and a single-gender mixed-ability partner. Call them A, B and C and you can just display the working partner on the board at the start of the lesson so as they come in they sit down in the designated pairings. NB the friendship pair is likely to be your ability pairing. For more focused Attainment Level work you could have a list of an addition fourth pairing who work together periodically.

PAIR WORK INTO GROUP WORK

I think that pair work is a much more effective learning tool than group work. In group work it is easier for one or two students to opt out and let the others do the work. However group work is of course important to the development of social and teamwork skills. I recommend that when you engage in group work then always go through a pair work step and join these pairs to make groups of four. Students will gel better and participate more equally in the task. The group is now two sets of pairs rather than four individuals thrown cold into the activity.

When planning a programme of study I suggest to schools that they also **plan for the frequency of Learning Partner and group work**. I have developed a list of suggested ratios across subjects which I present later on in this book.

ROTATION
Rotate the boy-girl seating partners every half-term or so that students sit and work in different combinations. Monitor carefully to ensure that students are happy and get on with who they sit and work with.

TEACH IT!

Children (and many adults!) need to be taught how to work effectively with partners and in teams. Here are some multi-adaptable ideas I have used with students to help teach them to listen to and share ideas with one-another.

Adapt the processes to the lesson content and use them as starters for a few minutes just before your Learning Partner and group work tasks. You will find that the students work together much better

GROUP WORK DEVELOPMENT IDEAS

It is always useful to practise the method of working itself, briefly, before using the process technique on the lesson content. So underneath each in italics I suggest an entertaining "way in" to teaching the process:

THE BASIC BRAINSTORM

Everyone quickly calls out ideas. These are not discussed: just written up by one group member.

What are the similarities between a cat and a refrigerator?

THE STRUCTURED BRAINSTORM

Everyone calls out ideas <u>in turn</u> around the circle. Everyone must contribute something. No argument or discussion is allowed.

What would happen if gravity stopped for ten seconds each and every day?"

"Around the group in turn" is especially good as a starting activity to get everyone involved in a discussion.

THAT'S IMPORTANT BECAUSE...
(THE AFFIRMATION BRAINSTORM, STAGE ONE)
Prior to making their own contribution each child must affirm the previous one that has bean made.
"Boys will be banned from school unless..."
Example
Pupil One: Boys will be banned from school unless they learn to listen better.
Pupil Two: That's important because if you don't listen then you won't know what to do. Boys will be banned from school unless they behave better...
Pupil Three: That's important because...

THE AFFIRMATION BRAINSTORM (STAGE TWO)
After one participant presents an idea they then point to another member of the group *at random,* who must first affirm this idea before presenting a new one.

The affirmation system, especially in sequence, is very useful in getting pupils to listen to one another's ideas and thus to actively teach listening skills. The problem with group work discussion is that we are so intent on working out what we want to say that we don't really listen to other people's contributions. Here the children have to because another participant's idea is their starting point.

THE PROS, CONS, AND INTERESTING POINTS METHOD
Each person in the group decides on a role and regardless of personal opinions must argue in that role. Pros must argue for the idea, Cons against and Interesting Points people merely reflect upon the issue (amusingly perhaps!) without coming down either for or against it. Again go around the

group in turn. No other arguments are allowed! Swap roles after first and second rounds.

It would be better to live life backwards, being born aged 75 and gradually getting younger rather than older!

This is especially good for teaching speculative thinking skills. It is also useful in getting students to explore alternative viewpoints to their own. They might have to argue against something they agree with for example and thus see things from another perspective.

COURTROOM

One person defends an idea, another attacks it. The other two are the judges. They are not allowed to express an opinion but have to ask lots of questions. The judges then make the final decision.

Let's all leave school now and go to the seaside!

Good for getting people to practise speaking in support of and against ideas. Especially good for action planning.

METAPHOR (STAGE ONE)

Before telling the group the subject for discussion, ask each to think of a noun (any object or animal will do).

Tell them to go around the group and say what their chosen word is.

Introduce your theme and tell the group that they are to use their noun as a metaphor for the subject and to explain it. For example, the word "building" had been chosen and your theme of "change." Then the student must begin their sentence "Change is a building because..." and complete the idea.

This idea is useful in developing creative thinking.

METAPHOR (STAGE TWO)
The group choose one metaphor and everyone explains it in turn.

PICTORIAL METAPHOR/SIMILE
The teacher chooses an appropriate pictorial metaphor for the conceptual elements of a lesson.

Each group is given an A3 photocopy of the picture (or different pictures). Working in a group, they then annotate it or adapt it to explore the concept.

"Here's a drawing of a house... show me how this is like the way a baby grows up."

ABSTRACT SHOPPING
Around the group in turn each pupil says "I went to the shops to buy" and inserts a concept, skill or consideration rather than an object.

"In order to get on well with other people I went to the shops to buy... tolerance!"

CHARACTER ROLES
Each person in turn adopts a character and relates what *this person* would say or think about an issue, for example Mum, Dad, Teacher etc.

"About you not doing your homework!"

RELEVANCE
Finally, of course, before you do anything with children communicate the relevance: tell them *why* you are doing it.
The ideas above are designed:

To help, students to develop their communication and group work skills.

To facilitate everyone being comfortable about making a contribution. This is achieved through creating common structures/ rules under which everyone operates: especially when the added rule of "no argument" is enforced.

To help students to develop their listening skills. Again the structures help, especially in the affirmation brainstorms and in the in-role brainstorms: the former helping to create empathy and the latter generating additional interest through the character being played.

For fun! To illustrate that sharing views and ideas can be fun as well as being important to our own understandings and our understanding of others.

****

Hey, let's not forget with all this pedagogy that above all else boys and girls just want to have fun. Let's make their learning fun!

Strategies for Outstanding Teaching (6)

ESTABLISH LEARNING PARTNERS

Objectives
To improve the "variety diet" in the classroom
To enhance and develop communication skills
To develop core literacy and numeracy skills
To develop autonomy in learning and to teach learning skills
To improve student/student relationship, enhance and develop social skills and thus sustain a safe and respectful learning environment

Each student is allocated three learning partners:
A learning partner of the opposite sex with whom they sit. Or, in the case of gender imbalance in the classroom, a same-sex partner who is allocated by the teacher so that this pairing is *mixed-ability*
A learning partner selected by the student (friendship and thus likely to be *similar ability*).
A learning partner of the same or opposite sex and *similar learning style preference*.

These Learning Partners (and seating partners) are changed every half-term.

Increase the level of proximal learning so that the learning partners function in rotation and/or suited to curriculum content. By the removal or a worksheet or text book, for example, you can ensure that the task is enacted together. Students could work forwards in their exercise book for individual work and backwards for partner work.
By giving A/B differing roles you can ensure equal participation: e.g. *A* reads out loud and *B* makes notes.
Use Learning Partners for:
Paired reading (and continue this practice throughout age-range).
Paired writing: creating written pieces together with, for example, both devising and both writing as they devise; or one devising and the other scribing.
Creating diagrams, drawings and notes together.
Doing mathematical operations together.

Extend Partner Learning into *Partner Teaching*:

At the start of the lesson for revision when, for example, *A* has revised a topic to teach *B* and *B* has revised a different topic to teach *A*.

At the end of the lesson when, in plenary, each is allocated to explain a different aspect of something learnt during that lesson.

In revision and at other times, the learning partners, working together, are allocated different topics to teach the rest of the class in groups of six

In Maths and English especially it is recommended that learning partners are used at least every third lesson and rotated across the three types.

After each Partner Learning or Teaching activity, students record who they have worked with through signature on sheet in their exercise book and monitor skills used. Merits are used to reward good effort and work specifically during these activities.

CHAPTER FIVE Use Descriptive-Reflective-Speculative

As part of a variety of approaches yet *consistently* use Descriptive-Reflective-Speculative sequencing to plan your lessons. This facilitates the delivery of an outstanding lesson, which (no surprise now to the reader!) has five key components to it.

THE OUTSTANDING LESSON

The outstanding lesson is a challenging lesson, with clearly defined learning objectives, taught to the top of the class (the highest level of attainment) rather than the middle It enables sequentially extending times on task rather than block timing. It balances the more formal teaching aspects with the students consolidating their learning at each step through "doing." It allows for appropriate differentiation by task. And the outstanding lesson facilitates the students presenting their gains in understandings.

The best lesson will have between three and five steps to it. Less than three steps and the teacher will probably not satisfy the needs of the average learner and, almost certainly, fail with the lower attainer. More than five steps and it is likely to be too "bitty" and lack cohesion.

Here's the plan that I shall then explain step-by-step…

THE OUTSTANDING LESSON
LEARNING OBJECTIVES ARE DISPLAYED
COMMUNICATE CHALLENGE
COMMUNICATE RELEVANCE
COMMUNICATE THE GAINS IN LEARNING

STEP ONE: STARTER

STEP TWO: DESCRIPTIVE ACTIVITY
                 TEACH DESCRIPTIVELY

STEP THREE: REFLECTIVE ACTIVITY
                 TEACH REFLECTIVELY

STEP FOUR: CENTRAL LEARNING ACTIVITY

STEP FIVE: STUDENTS PRESENT THEIR UNDERSTANDINGS

DEBRIEF GAINS IN LEARNING

Now let me show you how a lesson can move through these steps. I shall use the example of the Year-9 lesson on drugs that I cited in chapter one.

THE OUTSTANDING LESSON

DISPLAY YOUR LEARNING OBJECTIVES
Please see the Lesson Planning Template that follows this chapter

COMMUNICATE CHALLENGE
COMMUNICATE RELEVANCE
COMMUNICATE THE GAINS IN LEARNING

You are going to find today's lesson difficult. You will be able to do it but you are really going to have to think deeply and communicate well with others.

Drug taking is an issue that in some way is likely to affect us all. Today you are going to learn lots of new things about drugs. Things you really ought to know if you are to make sensible decisions for yourself.

STEP ONE: STARTER

Here are three photos of drugs commonly available: have a look- can you guess what they are?

STEP TWO: DESCRIPTIVE ACTIVITY
              TEACH DESCRIPTIVELY

I am going to give you and your partner just one sheet of paper between you and you have just five minutes. Talking with one-another write down ten things you would think of as being drugs. Go.

Well done.
Let me tell you now what the law says an "Unlawful Substance" is. Listen careful because your next task is to quickly tick the things on your list that are Unlawful Substances.

Two minutes... go quickly down your list and tick the Unlawful Substances on it.

STEP THREE: REFLECTIVE ACTIVITY
              TEACH REFLECTIVELY

Now take one of the Unlawful Substances that you ticked. Draw a column down the page. With your partner, and this is really difficult… can you think of five good things and five bad things about this drug?

Let me now take a drug that is readily available and give you some information about its good and bad effects.

STEP FOUR: CENTRAL LEARNING ACTIVITY

With your partner join up with another pair to form a group of four. In your group you are going to explore one of three important issues on which I am going to ask you to report back to the class. You have just fifteen minutes to complete your assignment before telling us what you have discovered.

Task One: Here's some information about marijuana. You have to tell us some facts about this drug and tell us why the drug is popular.
(YOU MIGHT DIFFERENTIATE THESE TASKS- FOR LOWER ATTAINERS: THINK DESCRIPTIVE EXTEND REFLECTIVE)*
Task Two: A girl goes to a party and takes Ecstasy. Why does she do it? If she were to do it, is there a way she could make sure that she does it more safely? Here's some information about the drug and about drug safety. In fifteen minutes time you will be telling us your findings.
(-FOR AVERAGE ATTAINERS: REFLECTIVE EXTEND TO SPECULATIVE)
Task Three: Here's some statistics about drug taking and young people. Find out the "drugs of preference" for young people of your age, select one, tell us a major problem it causes and tell us some ways we might overcome this problem.
(-FOR HIGH ATTAINERS: SPECULATIVE BUT CONSOLIDATE REFLECTIVE)
* See below.

STEP FIVE: STUDENTS PRESENT THEIR UNDERSTANDINGS

One group presents on each of the tasks whilst others make additional points.

DEBRIEF GAINS IN LEARNING

Well done everyone. Let me conclude by reminding you of some important points from today's lesson...

Let me now debrief you!

TEACHING TO THE TOP

Step One, the Starter, presents a visual input and a quick challenge to get the students focused

Step Two, the descriptive step starts with the students' own understandings. The instruction "find ten things you would think of as drugs" is challenging. The time is structured and after the five minutes perhaps the highest attainers have found their ten drugs. Perhaps the middle attainers have found seven, and the lowest attainers just three. It doesn't matter! The next instruction draws the class level again: "select one of your drugs" (One from ten, one from seven, one from three.) Everyone in the class has something to take on to the next step.

After **Step Three, the reflective step**: "find five good things and five bad things" the high attainers have maybe five good and five bad, the middle attainers three good things and three bad and the low attainers just one good and one bad. Again it doesn't matter because the next instruction is "select one of the bad things."

At each step the class is brought level but importantly all children are extended through the important hierarchy of Descriptive-Reflective-Speculative.

The low attainer frequently needs to extend their thinking skills from being simply descriptive. The mid range attainer needs to enhance and develop their reflective skills and together with the low attainer is likely to need to extend their thinking into the speculative dimension. The pairwork triggers the proximal learning and the children help one another to think and communicate through this mutually extending process.

And remember that boys especially need to develop their reflective skills.

SEQUENTIALLY EXTENDING TIMES ON TASK

D-R-S is a highly useful system for naturally extending the task time as the lesson progresses. Descriptive activities take the least time, reflective activities longer and speculative ones longer still. The first task facilitated short quick involvement with immediate outcomes, that is: immediate gratification for the boys!

Notice, as well, how the lesson developed the group work through a pair work step.

The timings? Step One, five minutes. Step Two, seven minutes. Step Three, eleven or so minutes, Step Four, fifteen minutes. Step Five, twenty minutes.

TEACHING AND DOING

At each step in the lesson there is a learning element taught at precisely the correct moment for it to be understood and, indeed, remembered.

The class is thinking descriptively and then the teacher extends their thinking by teaching descriptively.

By descriptive, I mean what something is or how to do something.

The class then thinks reflectively and then the more reflective learning element is introduced. The analysis is presented to minds ready to receive it!

By reflective, I mean why something is as it is or why I do what I do in the way that I do it.

Speculative thinking is "if."

By speculative activities, I mean: if I know what something is or how to do something and I know why this something is how it is or why I do what I do; then how can I apply this understanding to the new concept or approach? I suggest that the use of skills and understandings in a new context is a broadly speculative activity and fundamentally important in learning: since it is the application of learning that consolidates and extends it.

I'll leave you to grapple with and speculate upon that last paragraph!

DIFFERENTIATION*

The drugs lesson illustrates another use for D-R-S: to differentiate by task.

To me, effective differentiation by task is about giving groups appropriate tasks that, within the same time span, deliver *similar gains in learning.*

There is no need to take the D-R-S labels too literally. You will find that a broad understanding of these terms and the sequence will suffice in helping to plan your lessons.

PRESENTING BACK

This lesson has three learning components rather than just one because of the three differing tasks that are set. In presenting back, the students are demanded to communicate their new understandings. To do this they have to put them in order and to express them clearly and concisely. You are thus helping the boys to develop their linear process skills. In reporting back to the class what they have learnt, the students are learning through teaching. And the students are teaching one another. You can now assess their gains in learning.

Think D-R-S and you have a template for planning some highly dynamic and challenging lessons. A final point. Plan backwards! Think what are my gains in learning for this lesson? Next think of a really interesting group work activity to realise these gains. And now think "how am I going to get the class prepared for this group work activity?" Answer... through three pair work steps: in turn, descriptive, reflective and speculative.

HOMEWORK
Select a key lesson that you are soon to teach. Plan it and deliver it using the Excellent Lesson.

*I consider that a lot of so-called differentiation is useless! Good step by step teaching overcomes learning disadvantages. Effective differentiation is seldom achieved through group work. Here it simply sets a ceiling for student attainment: a self-fulfilling prophecy like setting which limits expectations for both teachers and students. The most effective differentiation is achieved one-to-one by the teacher focusing on the needs of an individual student.
In my opinion, setting is the biggest perpetrator of inequality on Working Class children: you might as well stamp a child's postal code on their forehead at birth- this will tell you what set to put them in at school!*

Strategies for Outstanding Teaching (7)

USE DESCRIPTIVE-REFLECTIVE-SPECULATIVE SEQUENCING IN LESSON STRUCTURES

Objectives

To improve the quality of step-by-step teaching

To clarify and sequence clear steps for the learners

To improve the quality of interactional teaching and the quality/quantity of experiential learning.

STEP ONE Starter *5 minutes*

Display learning objectives which should be clear, concise and express learning through D-R-S from the students' perspective.

Learning Objectives might be

D In this lesson I will learn how to......

R I will understand why.......

S I will be able to apply this/evaluate this in.....

Strategy link: use D component as "Learning/Revision Tick List"

Talk through Learning Objective and communicate challenge.

STEP TWO *10 minutes*

Part 1 Descriptive Teaching

Through interactional whole-class teaching, teach How to do something or What something is. Facilitate the class in describing something.

Part 2 Descriptive Doing

Task the students to do something on their own or with a partner to consolidate/practise how to do something or to clarify what the something is or to delineate the description of the something.

Strategy link: use "Go For Five" steps in doing and find five descriptive points.

Strategy link: use "Think-Communicate-Write"

STEP THREE *15 minutes*

Part 1 Reflective Teaching

Through interaction whole-class teaching Explain Why the something is done in the way it is done or Why the something is as it is.

Part 2 Reflective Doing
Task the students in a task that explores the concept under-
pinning the understanding of how to do the something or what
the something is.
Use kinaesthetic and visual approaches that firmly establish
relevance to the students' own world and experiences.
Strategy link: use "Go For Five" to explain why.
INTERACTIVE MINI PLENARY
"So far we have learnt how to…. and explored why we…."

STEP FOUR *15 minutes*
Central Learning Activity
Individually, in pairs or in groups of no more than four formed by
previous pairing the students are tasked to extend their
understandings speculatively through applying or evaluating
these understandings in new contexts.

STEP FIVE *10 minutes* Students show off their learning
Plenary in which the students *explain, illustrate, enact, and show-
off* their learning to the whole class or to other pairings or other
groups. Followed by teacher plenary.
Strategy link: use "Partner Teaching".

Additional Resources
Lesson Planning Templates

I have developed these templates as an electronic version to minimalise the amount of work for teachers. They are aimed at developing a "house-style" of working within Departments and/or within the whole school.

Once the lesson plans are cut and pasted then saved to computer, they provide a simple template for teachers to fill in and save and *gradually* build up a complete set of lesson plans for individual and team use. They might be completed initially for key lessons, perhaps working together as a team. The emphases for the constituent components are linked to my methodology described in this book, (proximal partner learning; descriptive-reflective-speculative sequencing; think-communicate write; read –think-communicate; sharing what has been learnt etc.) you may, of course, present your own emphases in a similar format.

I consider that a resource of clearly drafted lesson plans is a key element for the consistent delivery of Outstanding Teaching and for providing an exciting and varied learning diet to students.

Electronic versions of these are available- please contact me on geoff.hannan@btinternet.com...

PROGRAMME OF STUDY *Fill in and cut and paste to all lessons in this PoS and below for projection in classroom.*
LESSON NUMBER: CLASS:
SUBJECT OF LESSON: ATTAINMENT LEVEL[S]: *Fill in and cut and paste below for projection in the classroom.*

LEARNING OBJECTIVES: *Fill in the objectives and cut and paste below for projection in the classroom and for students' learning checklists*

DIFFERENTIATION: *Fill in the names of students with SEN and on the G&T register and note an additional teaching input for each.*

This lesson's method:
During this lesson your will be working:

- Individually
- With your boy/girl learning partner
- With your friendship learning partner
- With your learning styles learning partner
- In small groups

Embolden *the central method you will be using and cut and paste below for projection in the classroom.*

CORE SKILLS
WRITING EMPHASIS
Writing type:
- Note taking
- Diagram making
- Short sentence
- Extended writing

TYPE OF WRITING
- INDIVIDUALLLY
- WITH PARTNER
- WITH GROUP

Embolden *the main writing type and process to be used. Cut and paste below for projection.*

CORE SKILLS
READING EMPHASIS
Reading purpose:
- Find information
- Reinforce learning
- Extend understandings

TYPE OF READING
- INDIVIDUALLY
- PAIRED READING
- READING IN GROUPS

Embolden *the main purpose and process to be used. Cut and paste below for projection.*

INTRODUCTION
Relevance:
Challenge:

STEP ONE STARTER: DURATION:
RESOURCE REFERENCE:

STEP TWO [Descriptive/What/How]
TEACHING STEP:
ACTIVITY: DURATIION:
RESOURCE REFERENCE;

STEP THREE [Reflective/Why/Analysis/Concept]
TEACHING STEP:
ACTIVITY: DURATIION:
RESOURCE REFERENCE;

MINI PLENARY
Check for understandings of especially:
Traffic Light

STEP FOUR [Central Leaning Activity: Speculative]
INSTRUCTION:
ACTIVITY: DURATIION:
RESOURCE REFERENCE;

STEP FIVE: SHARING THE LEARNING
TO PARTNER- BETWEEN PARTNERS- WITHIN
GROUPS-BETWEEN GROUPS *Embolden which*   DURATION

FINAL PLENARY
Check for understandings of especially:
Traffic Light

Lesson Planning Template

PROGRAMME OF STUDY:
LESSON NUMBER: CLASS:
SUBJECT OF LESSON: ATTAINMENT LEVEL[S]:

LEARNING OBJECTIVES:

DIFFERENTIATION:

This lesson's method:
During this lesson your will be working:

- Individually
- With your boy/girl
  learning partner
- With your friendship
  learning partner
- With your learning styles
  learning partner
- In small groups

INTRODUCTION
Relevance:
Challenge:

CORE SKILLS
WRITING EMPHASIS
Writing type:
- Note taking
- Diagram making
- Short sentence
- Extended writing

TYPE OF WRITING
- INDIVIDUALLLY
- WITH PARTNER
- WITH GROUP

CORE SKILLS
READING EMPHASIS
Reading purpose:
- Find information
- Reinforce learning
- Extend
  understandings

TYPE OF READING
- INDIVIDUALLY
- PAIRED READING
- READING IN
  GROUPS

STEP ONE STARTER: DURATION:
RESOURCE REFERENCE:

STEP TWO [Descriptive/What/How]
TEACHING STEP:
ACTIVITY: DURATIION:
RESOURCE REFERENCE;

STEP THREE [Reflective/Why/Analysis/Concept]
TEACHING STEP:
ACTIVITY: DURATIION:
RESOURCE REFERENCE;

MINI PLENARY
Check for understandings of especially:
Traffic Light

STEP FOUR [Central Leaning Activity: Speculative]
INSTRUCTION:
ACTIVITY: DURATIION:
RESOURCE REFERENCE;

STEP FIVE: SHARING THE LEARNING
TO PARTNER- BETWEEN PARTNERS- WITHIN
GROUPS-BETWEEN GROUPS

                                                        DURATION

FINAL PLENARY
Check for understandings of especially:
Traffic Light

Lesson Planning Template

Welcome to today's lesson!

PROGRAMME OF STUDY:
LESSON NUMBER:
TODAY'S SUBJECT:

THE LEARNING OBJECTIVES:

LEARNING METHOD:
WRITING EMPHASIS:
READING EMPHASIS:

SPECIAL MERITS FOR:

Classroom Display Template

CHAPTER SIX Action Writing:
Think-Communicate-Write

We learn nothing just BY writing. Writing expresses previous understanding. For writing to be effective in learning the understanding needs to precede it. Just as oracy precedes literacy so should thinking and understanding precede writing. Thus writing becomes a tool for expressing and consolidating learning. Boys have weaker verbal skills than girls. Boys have poorer reflective skills than girls. Boys find the dynamics of writing more difficult and writing may actually become a block to their learning. Consider any child with poor literacy skills. He or she spends so much time thinking about the formation of words and sentences that they may easily lose the threads of the ideas they are trying to communicate on the page. To so many students writing becomes a boring, passive chore that they are forced into doing. The fun of a learning activity may be easily spoilt by having to write it up. Of course writing is highly important and with a little imagination and the enactment of the tenets previously explored, writing too may become more boy-friendly and student-friendly as a learning activity

I remind you of some previously made points. **Structure on-task talk.** If something is talked through prior to it being written it is written and understood better. So, as part of your varied diet of activities in the classroom, structure time so that children talk through their gain in learning and at the end of the lesson prior to writing it down. Writing as a tool for learning should follow the sequence **THINK-COMMUNICATE-WRITE.**

Now, here are some ideas that you will find improve the quality of your students' writing...

DECONSTRUCT IT

Firstly, **develop a "hit list" of key words** in your subject and find ways to get students playing with these words so that they learn them and can use them appropriately. Have quizzes more frequently, for example: five of these key words and their meanings learnt for homework and a quick quiz the following day. Have word searches with these key words available for use at the end of the some lesson. Introduce new words by a quick word search activity at the start of the lesson As you read to the class ask them to listen out for key words and expressions and to make a quick note of them. Before they write put some words and expressions on the board and instruct the class to use them in what they write. Use the "that is" technique:

"When you use the words that I have put on the backboard you have to explain them simply, ask your partner to help... Today we learnt about osmosis, that is..."

Use flashcards and posters. Devise a poster in the form of a diagram with your key words and put it on the wall. Challenge individual students to come to the front of the class, point to a word and explain it. Boys, especially, like writing on the white board so challenge students to come up and write these important words in front of the class. Play memory challenges and adding games with your subject's vocabulary.

"Partner A says a word, B repeats it and adds another word, then A repeats both the words and adds a third, and so on. Let's see who gets the longest list of these important words!"

After actively teaching the words of your subject develop from phrase stems through sentence stems into paragraph stems. Let me show you what I mean by using the desert island and the mirror example from Chapter Two.

"With your partner see if you can find five uses of a mirror for survival on a desert island, here... use this sheet to write your ideas down... you have just two minutes!"

1. to_____
2. to_____
3. to_____
4. to_____
5. to_____

The word "to" demands them to use the verb stem and to write down the participle appropriately: "to signal" rather than just a single word response "signalling".

"Now as I ask you to tell me your ideas use the word "to" in your reply and answer me in a short sentence. I am asking you to do this because it helps you to express your ideas better especially when you come to writing them on paper. OK John... tell us one of your uses for this mirror.
John: To signal.
Make it a sentence, John... "You..."
John: You could use a mirror to signal.
Well done! Good idea!"

See what I mean? Having been through this precise deconstructional and verbal process when they come to write about the desert island and mirror their written expression will improve considerably and they will remember the ideas better as well.

The next step in this process gives you a very simple and effective way of extending the students' writing.

TEACH CONNECTIVES

"Now I want you to select one of your survival uses of a mirror and find five steps for using it. Write your steps down on this sheet..."

First_____.
Secondly_____.
Next_____.
Then_____.
Finally_____.

"Well done. Now as I ask you for your five steps you have to respond in a full paragraph using the linking words on your sheet. John... give it a try...how would you use a mirror to signal?
First you go to high ground. Secondly you flash the mirror at the sun. Next you look to see if the ship has seen it. Then you use code to send a message. Finally you look for instructions. Excellent, well done!

And well done teacher! With verbal expression preceding written expression you have taught little Johnny <u>how</u> to write.

You will find "first, secondly, next, then and finally" a very effective tool to develop especially boys' extended writing and also to teach them to sequence things.

If you wish to get them to illustrate teach them to use:
compared with
in the same way
equally
similarly
as well as

If you wish to get them to contrast teach them to use:
however
but
on the one hand, on the other
yet
although

If you wish to get them to persuade:
obviously
of course
clearly
surely
certainly

To give an opinion:
It would seem that
possibly
maybe
perhaps
definitely

To write about cause and effect, then:
thus
as a result of
so therefore
because
in order to

To conclude a piece of writing, teach them the words they need to close it:
In conclusion, finally, in the end, on the whole, in summary, boys especially need to be shown how to use writing as a tool!

TEACH D-R-S

You will find that actively teaching especially boys how to write will deliver excellent results. A good piece of written work will follow the sequence Descriptive-Reflective-Speculative just like a good lesson. Teach the class to use the hierarchy. I advocate the use of a classroom poster and/or a printed copy of the following for each child that ever has to write anything!

USE
DESCRIPTIVE
REFLECTIVE
SPECULATIVE

FIRST
DESCRIBE THE SCENE
EXPLAIN THE FACTS
EXPLAIN THE SEQUENCE OR STEPS IN DOING SOMETHING

THEN
EXPLAIN THE FEELINGS
EXPLAIN THE CONSEQUENCES
EXPLAIN THE RESULT

FINALLY
DRAW CONCLUSIONS
PRESENT NEW IDEAS
SPECULATE UPON POSSIBILITIES

THINK, COMMUNICATE AND WRITE D-R-S

Strategies for Outstanding Teaching (8)

Writing
Use Think-Communicate-Write

Develop a hit list of key words and terms.

Duplicate and distribute the lists.

Display key words and expressions as part of your learning objectives.

Have word challenges with the students on meanings and spellings.

Engage in Partner and Group Challenges as well as individually.

Display the words in the classroom.

Request students memorise them in groups of five.

Teach connectives.

Use connectives verbally prior to using them in writing.

Teach and use Descriptive-Reflective-Speculative sequencing and request students follow it consistently in their writing.

Reading
Use Read-Think-Communicate

Read for purpose, especially:
- to find information
- to consolidate learning

Use paired reading: request students read out loud to their partner so that all students are reading together periodically and consistently.

Teach scanning and skimming techniques

Use the above in all curriculum areas

CHAPTER SEVEN Action Reading: Read-Think-Communicate

For writing to enrich learning the sequence is Think-Communicate-Write. Reading as a tool for learning follows the sequence READ-THINK-COMMUNICATE.

Girls and boys tend to read quite differently. Boys read material directly related to their interests and, broadly speaking, for the purpose of acquiring information and factual detail. Girls will read anything as long as it is about people and their relationships! Girls read from start to finish whilst boys "skip read" even to the extent of starting the book at chapter five. If a boy is getting bored, he will readily miss a few pages and jump to a bit he finds more interesting. He is more likely to skim the book first and be drawn into reading through pictures and diagrams. I suspect that the bedside table of most men will hold two books: one on politics, a biography or similar book related to their interests and a travel book. Their shelves are likely to be filled by books that have been partly read!

With boys especially it is important for the teacher to give them a clear brief. Tell them why you are asking them to read a particular thing and define a purpose for the reading. The more precise you can make it the better for the pupils.

READING FOR PURPOSE

Ask pupils to read for the purpose of finding information which they are then going to use:

"You have ten minutes to read chapter one about the Victorians. Quickly jot down any information you find on agriculture during this historic period. Then select five important details from your list. I'm then going to ask you to tell me what they are and to explain why you think they are important pieces of information." (DESCRIPTIVE-REFLECTIVE).

REINFORCEMENT

Periodically, prior to the introduction of new content get the pupils to read to consolidate the things that they have learnt so far:

"Firstly I want you to read in pairs and in turn to one-another the way that Hans asked Gita the way to the station, then we will be finding some new ways of giving people directions."

INTERACTION THROUGH SPECULATION

Meaning and understanding is a synthesis of what the writer writes and the reader or learner brings to the text themselves. With boys it is important to overtly activate this relationship. Think speculate and you have a boy-friendly reading activity:

"Read just paragraph one and then turn your book over. What do you think happens next?"

"What do you think will happen when the flower is put into the liquid nitrogen?"

Don't give them the answer, instead:
"Now read on and discover whether or not you are correct."
Or, for example:
"As you read about Jane imagine that you are her! When you get to the end of the page, stop reading and jot down a few words to describe how you would feel in Jane's position."

READ TO RECORD INFORMATION

Provide headings on the blackboard or a worksheet and instruct the students to make word notes under each heading as they read:
"Read chapter one about France for homework and make notes under the headings on your worksheet. Tomorrow you are going to be travellers returning from the country and you are going to be interviewed on television about what you have learnt from your trip."
And go for five!

TRAVELLER'S NOTES

THE TERRAIN
1
2
3
4
5
THE CLIMATE
1
2
3
4
5

THE PEOPLE

1

2

3

4

5

THE EXPORTS

1

2

3

4

5

THE IMPORTS

1

2

3

4

5

CRITICAL READING

Reading can become a significant way to extend boys' reflective thinking skills.

"As you read this piece use your worksheet to jot down some ways in which you agree with the writer and some ways in which you disagree. See if you can find five points of agreement and five points of disagreement. Later we will be using this sheet to have a full-scale debate on the issues."

"One of you read the chapter to your group. Whilst you are listening to the reader, one of you note down some arguments against what the writer is saying. Another note down ways in which the writer is showing bias. The fourth: see if you can find examples of the way in which the writer is being sexist!"

"Read the section in turn around the group and then as a group see if you can find five things that you disagree with."

READING TO TEACH

Many boys like to show off! Capitalise upon it and you have a neat way of covering a lot of information quickly:

"This is an activity called EXPERTS. It works like this: you have just fifteen minutes to read a different section of the book each making notes and then you are going to become the expert and teach the rest of your group what you have discovered. They are going to then take notes from you and this way everyone will have learnt a lot."

"I'm going to divide the class up into six groups. Each group is going to have a different section/chapter to read. Each group should read their section taking turns and then make one set of notes on it. Then, in turn you are going to teach the class about your section, whilst they, in their turn take notes".

PAIRED READING

Rather than you reading to the class, think "Is there an opportunity here to develop literacy skills?" Pupils reading quietly to one another in pairs is an excellent way to improve their skills. Begin this process young and by getting them to read their *own homework* to one-another. If a child is writing something for the purpose of reading it to another child they will take more care over the piece of work. As well as consolidating the learning in reading to one another they will also be correcting any mistakes they find. Add the "experts" idea where the listening partner makes notes and you are on to a real motivational winner with boys!

Remember also that it doesn't matter a jot what a child reads as long as they read! With boys especially, if they are interested in a specific topic then this may be used with great effect to develop their interest and skills in reading itself. Literacy Skills development is not the responsibility of the English Department. It is a cross-curricular imperative. The best results in developing reading and writing skills with boys who find it difficult will come in boy-friendly areas of the curriculum. Hit literacy skills development through science and technology! And use a varied approach so that all children within a certain time frame have all the reading opportunities that they can. Here they are!

VARIETY CHECKLIST

ACTION	PURPOSE	INTERACTION
Teacher reads to class		
	Reinforcement	
	To speculate	
	To be critical	
	To record information	
	For fun	
		Pupils follow
		Pupils make notes
Pupils read to one-another in pairs		
Pupils read their homework to one-another in pairs		
	Reinforcement	
	To speculate	
	To be critical	
	To record information	
	For fun	
	Listener makes notes	
		Pair to teach other pair/ pair to teach class

ACTION	PURPOSE	INTERACTION
One pupil reads to small group		
Pupils read in turn around the group		
	Reinforcement	
	To speculate	
	To be critical	
	To record information	
	For fun	
		Listeners make notes together and prioritise.
		Each listener has something specific to listen for.
		Groups teach class.
Individual pupils read to class (good readers only!)		
	Reinforcement	
	To speculate	
	To be Critical	
	To record information	
	For fun	
		All make notes
		Groups listen out for specifics

OUT-LOUD READING

Reading out-loud is a fine way to develop reading skills. To encourage boys to read out loud, be it their own work or from a book, first ask them to read to one-another in pairs. It is also a good idea to give them some time to rehearse their readings prior to reading out loud. A useful homework assignment, for example, could be to practise reading a section of a book out loud because next lesson they will be reading it to the class.

READING SKILLS

Take some time to actively teach reading strategies. Introduce and teach the skills involved through high challenge games. Teach your pupils *to scan* for specific information by running their fingers down the right hand side of the page and look for certain words. When they see a word then tell them to read the sentence that contains it. Teach them how *to skim* for gist by running their fingers along the lines quickly, stopping and recalling the information they have taken in. And teach them occasionally to read intensively by holding their book up in front of them and read every word.

Try teaching them to punctuate accurately by asking them at times to say "comma, full stop," etcetera, whilst they read.

Some **15% of classroom "doing" time should be used in reading** in a variety of ways. Some **20% of doing time should be used in writing** in a variety of ways. *One usually sees far too little reading and way too much writing!*

CHAPTER EIGHT
Teach How-Think Ratios

How often do you think that Darren says to his mates "Hey guys, let's all go down the corner and analyse a poem?" Probably not a lot.

A great deal of learning is not rational, it is logical. So much of what we try to teach children runs counter-intuitive and contrary to their nature that *it* **needs to be taught**. This is an important point so I will press it. You need to be taught if you are to learn. Let me give an example of the counter intuitive nature of learning and the necessity for an "up-front" approach to teaching.

Imagine you have won a Game Show on T.V. The game host shows you three doors and she says to you "I know what's behind each of these doors and you don't. Behind two of them is a cabbage. Behind the third is a million pounds. Choose a door!"

You then select but are not allowed to open one of the doors.

She then opens one of doors that you haven't chosen and reveals a cabbage behind it. "Would you like to change your mind?" she now says, "If you wish to, you can now choose the last door instead of your original one."

Assuming you are not incredibly stupid and actually wish to win the cabbage, the question is, should you now change your original choice to the last door. Do you stand more chance of winning the million pounds that way? Think about it before you read on.

The answer is at the end of the chapter. You were probably wrong.

Why were you wrong? Probability is logical not rational. The mathematical reality of the world we live in runs counter-intuitive. We call our failure to grasp probability theory "Sod's Law." In a supermarket you are always in a slow queue. Well, you are likely to be. Five queues and you choosing one only gives you a one in five chance of being in the fastest. Your own personal, rational and intuitive world has no real need to understand the subtleties of probability mathematics. You would probably never rationally come up with the reasons behind its laws or, indeed, find it easy to accept that through changing your choice of door you double your chances of being a millionaire. It has to be taught to you. Darren needs to be taught poetry analysis.

"Reader, if you ever win a Game Show and are shown three doors and later a cabbage behind on of them, then given the choice, change your first decision."

"Class, here is a poem and my five steps of how to analyse it. Let me take you through each step and show you how it is done. Now, here's another poem. Using my steps see if you can crack the code of this poem. Work in pairs. Darren and Cindy work together. You have ten minutes, the clock starts now!"

TEACH HOW BEFORE WHY

In maths, the numbers define the concept. To understand the concepts of probability you have to first know how to use number. This is the way that learning works in many spheres to the student. If you wish to understand what caused the First World War you need to be taught how to understand it first through the application of cause and effect. Conceptual understanding fails if we do not give students the language and thinking tools to understand it. "This is how to think, now think this way in order to understand!" In simple terms in the classroom this means TEACH HOW BEFORE WHY.

Teach Descriptive before Reflective. I remind you of the outstanding lesson in chapter five. The Descriptive is what something is or HOW to do something. Look at one of your programmes of study. Think of the key "hows" in it and teach them overtly and sequentially using D-R-S and you will see a major improvement in your students' performance and *motivation*.

After all, one is likely to have little interest in knowing why I do what I can't do in the first place!

RATIOS

I suggest that there are three key ratios in learning management:

TEACHING TO DOING
INDIVIDUAL TO PROXIMAL
PRAISE TO REPRIMAND

The Teaching to Doing ratio is the proportion of time a teacher spends teaching the whole class to the amount of time the students spend on-task. The Individual to Proximal ratio is the amount of on-task time spent working individually to the amount of time spent working in a structured way in pairs or groups. And the Praise to Reprimand ratio is, and must never drop below, 4:1.

TEACHING TO DOING

In order to teach the many hows demanded in learning, the teaching to doing ratio needs to be pretty high. By teaching I mean, interactive and dynamic, step by step approaches such as illustrated in chapter five. As a broad rule of thumb, I give some examples below of how much time the teacher, I figure needs to teach in Key Stages 2 to 4. The first part of the ratio refers to amount of time the teacher spends addressing the whole class and the second, the amount of time the children are engaged in a *wide variety* of tasks.

TEACHING TO DOING RATIOS (first number is teaching, second is doing)

	KS2	KS3	KS4
MATHS	1 : 2	1 : 2	1 : 3
MODERN LANGUAGES	1 : 3	1 : 4	1 : 4
ENGLISH	1 : 3	1 : 3	1 : 4
SCIENCE	1 : 3	1 : 3	1 : 3
TECHNOLOGY	1 : 3	1 : 4	1 : 5
HISTORY	1 : 3	1 : 3	1 : 3
GEOGRAPHY	1 : 3	1 : 3	1 : 3

In English at KS2 this means, for example, that a one-hour lesson should consist of 15 minutes step-by-step, challenging and interactive whole-class teaching; consolidated and extended by 45 minutes of a variety of activities.

INDIVIDUAL TO PROXIMAL

There are two ways that children learn: on their own and together with other children thus the Doing ratio on the right above is then broken down into these two types of Doing.

INDIVIDUAL TO PROXIMAL LEARNING RATIOS

	(I : P) KS2	(I : P) KS3	(I : P) KS4
MATHS	1 : 2 (1:1)	1 : 2 (1:1)	1 : 3 (2:1)
MODERN LANG	1 : 3 (1:2)	1 : 4 (1:3)	
ENGLISH	1 : 3 (1:2)	1 : 3 (1:2)	1 : 4 (1:1)
SCIENCE	1 : 3 (1:2)	1 : 3 (1:2)	1 : 3 (1:2)
TECHNOLOGY	1 : 3 (2:1)	1 : 4 (3:1)	1 : 5 (4:1)
HISTORY	1 : 3 (1:2)	1 : 3 (1:2)	1 : 3 (2:1)
GEOGRAPHY	1 : 3 (1:2)	1 : 3 (1:2)	1 : 3 (2:1)

Thus in Maths in KS3, about half the *doing* time is done individually and half in pairs/groups. Rotating learning partners and working on a mathematical operation together proves an effective strategy for raising attainment

This isn't rocket science! You know your students and your subject. The ratio system is a tool for encouraging teachers to be a little more precise in translating pedagogy into classroom practice. **Make your own decision about what these ratios should be but THINK RATIOS** and you have a tool for improving children's performance.

FOUR TO ONE

To motivate students or modify their behaviour then the praise to reprimand ratio must never drop below 4:1 in favour of the former.

If in a lesson observation, you tick every time a teacher praises a class and every time a teacher tells off that class and the ratio drops below four to one then the teacher is beginning to have major control problems. If you tell off a child and you wish them to modify their behaviour then, after you tell them off, you must praise the appropriate behaviour if you wish to sustain it.

Try to ignore the negative behaviour whilst ensuring that you praise the positive, is frequently the best advice to give teachers.

****

The answer to the problem is if you change your original choice to the last door remaining then you *double* your chances of winning the million pounds!

Strategies for Outstanding Teaching (9)

TEACHING TO DOING RATIOS (first number is teaching, second is doing)

	KS2	KS3	KS4
MATHS	1 : 2	1 : 2	1 : 3
MODERN LANGUAGES	1 : 3	1 : 4	1 : 4
ENGLISH	1 : 3	1 : 3	1 : 4
SCIENCE	1 : 3	1 : 3	1 : 3
TECHNOLOGY	1 : 3	1 : 4	1 : 5
HISTORY	1 : 3	1 : 3	1 : 3
GEOGRAPHY	1 : 3	1 : 3	1 : 3

In English at KS2 this means, for example, that a one-hour lesson should consist of 15 minutes step-by-step, challenging and interactive whole-class teaching; consolidated and extended by 45 minutes of a variety of activities.

INDIVIDUAL TO PROXIMAL LEARNING RATIOS

	(I : P) KS2	(I : P) KS3	(I : P) KS4
MATHS	1 : 2 (1:1)	1 : 2 (1:1)	1 : 3 (2:1)
MODERN LANG	1 : 3 (1:2)	1 : 4 (1:3)	
ENGLISH	1 : 3 (1:2)	1 : 3 (1:2)	1 : 4 (1:1)
SCIENCE	1 : 3 (1:2)	1 : 3 (1:2)	1 : 3 (1:2)
TECHNOLOGY	1 : 3 (2:1)	1 : 4 (3:1)	1 : 5 (4:1)
HISTORY	1 : 3 (1:2)	1 : 3 (1:2)	1 : 3 (2:1)
GEOGRAPHY	1 : 3 (1:2)	1 : 3 (1:2)	1 : 3 (2:1)

Thus in Maths in KS3, about half the *doing* time is done individually and half in pairs/groups. Rotating learning partners and working on a mathematical operation together proves an effective strategy for raising attainment

For the ones who keep opening doors

CHAPTER NINE Outstanding Learning

A major part of my work for the last thirty-five years has been with children and young people directly; touring interactive learning programmes on themes as diverse as sex education to drugs awareness. With the current thrust towards raising standards much of my work with children and young people now is about the ways they can lift their own performance and do better in school. With this in mind I present in this chapter some ideas from my roadshows about how we learn things best.
You might like to help your children discover the strategies below....

In my Year-11 roadshow to help boost GCSE results I use a flashcard to illustrate a key point about learning. During a short comedy routine which I perform for them I flash a single word written on this card- guess what the word is!

Hi. I thought I would begin by doing something on the subject of *. Now, of course, the trouble sometimes with * is that * can be an embarrassing subject. Nevertheless I intend to take a totally open and uninhibited look at the entire subject of *. Now it's pretty obvious in looking at you that there are here today lots of *y people. Some who are perhaps *less but at some point in our lives any one of us might have *ual issues. Not enough * or too much *! Even * six times a day. So how might we deal with these * ual issues? Let me give you an example.

I once knew a *agenarian sailor from Es* who had an amazing way of dealing with his *ual issues by the use of a *tant. (And so on!)

My point? In order to make the comedy (such as it is!) work two things are needed: timing and mental activity. To get the jokes the mental insertion of the word had to be just at the right moment and you needed to make the effort of meeting the script halfway. A third point: the connections get more and more demanding of the audience as the routine progresses. It starts with a small amount of mental involvement and ends up with greater demands. I think there are good analogies here with learning and with effective teaching.

For your learning to take place then you need to interact in some way with what you are learning. Here are some ways you can do it....

THE BIG FIVE

- Variety: use several approaches to learning and memory. If you find something is not easily recalled one way then use a different technique on it.
- Ask "Do I understand this?" We recall things better if we can **explain** our understanding of them. This "reflective statement" is important to long term recall.
- Make up your own examples and explanations. Making learning personal aids our recall of information.
- Think in colourful pictures and shapes as well as words: we remember images better than concepts.
- Repetition, repetition, repetition! But do things in different ways to remember them better.

KEY STRATEGIES

Have a learning buddy! I recommend to teachers that as part of revising for exams they use the Learning Partner system explained in Chapter Four; specifically at the start of lessons leading up to the exams. The students are given a list of things to revise and a schedule of homework to revise them on specific dates. Students in the class then spend five minutes at the start of lessons teaching their partner what they have revised the night before. This proves a useful strategy to help them organise their revision but importantly it demands them to verbalise their learning. We recall things better if we communicate our learning to someone-else. Ironically, we learn best through teaching!

AT HOME

Be your child's Learning Partner especially during revision. Get them to explain what they have learnt to you. Be their student and get them to teach you how to do things and explain the Why behind things. In teaching you they will recall things better.

TOPIC LIST

The next thing I recommend is that you obtain or create a simple list of things you want to or have to learn. Schools should provide these to examination students. They should contain key words such as subject-specialist language and phrases and just a few bullet points of the main subsections within the topic. You can tick these off as you learn or revise them.

If you have a lot to revise then some form of prioritisation would be useful, such as putting *M* for Must and *S* for Should and *I* for if possible against the different elements.

Next, set a timetable for revision and stick to it.

TIME

I recommend that you should "chunk" learning down into twenty-minute sections. Do twenty minutes of revision, for example; have a short break; do a quick review out loud of what you have just learnt (this is where having your own tame student to teach comes in) and then proceed onto the next twenty minutes. I also suggest you learn three smallish topics/processes during one revision session and, as well as working as above, you should then revisit all three of them at the end of an hour.

What you must do is interact in someway with what you are learning. You have to put the * in.

There are basically four ways you can interact with learning and much will depend on your preferred learning style. I think you will probably need to use a mixture of each.

VISUAL LEARNERS

Visual Learners might prefer to transfer information onto mind maps in some way, for example using spider diagrams. My advice would be keep them as simple as possible to aid recall. Use no more that five branches and three sub-branches (See Chapter Two: Go for Five).

Also, be consistent across your mind maps, e.g. find five branches for each and use the same three colours. I suggest green for descriptive information (the grass roots of knowledge), yellow for the reflective information that explains why and expresses the concept of ideas around things (the sun that makes the grass grow) and red for the speculative, evaluative elements or the bits you find most difficult to recall (like the dawn of new ideas!)

Use highlighters as well especially when you revisit your mind maps.

EXPLAIN YOUR MIND MAPS OUTLOUD TO YOURSELF OR SOMEONE ELSE. You could use your mobile phone to photograph your mind maps so that you take them with you and can revise at odd moments. You could work together with your learning partner in developing mind maps and then swap them by attaching them to text messages.

You could scan mind maps to a computer and add a voice file that explains them. Next time you revisit the ideas, sit and observe the information as you listen to yourself explain it.

Other ideas that might work well for more visual learners are drawing stick cartoons to remember steps and sequences: again, I would advise no more than five.

You might like to use "rhyme keys" to remember lists. Here you first memorise a visual rhyme for each number from one to five: one is a bun; two is a shoe; three is a tree; four is a door; five is a beehive. What you want to remember gets visually attached in your memory to the item. Now think of your bun with a bottle of milk sticking out of it. Your shoe is stuffed with meat, fish and chicken legs. Behind the door are huge sacks containing grains and stuck on top of your beehive are an apple and a carrot. And what do you have? The basic food types: dairy, meat, grains, fruit and veg.

AUDITORY LEARNERS

Auditory Learners may learn best through hearing things and speaking about things. Talking through things is especially useful to people who prefer this learning style. Auditory learners should record their learning and listen to it played back. They might benefit from easy to recall acrostics to recall sequences: such as **E**very **G**ood **B**oy **D**eserves **F**un which might help you remember key progressions in music. If you are good at remembering names then you might like to invent acrostic names to remember, for example, the colours in a rainbow: let me introduce you to Roy G. Biv; he's a painter, you know! (Colours and their order in the spectrum). Think of a taxi smashing into a phone box and you will probably not forget the Spanish for a phone box: cabina (get it?)

Auditory learners may benefit from reading information out loud rather than just to themselves; since this way they are hearing it, as well as seeing it.

KINAESTHETIC

Kinaesthetic Learners will learn better through doing things. I suggest they explore using movement in their learning in some form or another. Cutting bits of information up and reassembling it in some way might help them to recall things (I use this idea in the Modern Language Template in Chapter Three). Walking through processes and using their bodies to make shapes could also be effective. Rather than just trying to learn the process of photosynthesis: walk through it and act out a plant growing as you use the words. Kinaesthetic learners may also recall individual terms that bit better if they attach a hand movement to them. For example take your forefinger and make a circular movement beside your head to remember the word "reflective." Generally speaking, Kinaesthetic Learners will recall things better if they can find ways of "doing them" as well as hearing them or seeing them. A nice example is again a humorous one-

Say the word gullible slowly enough and it sounds like "oranges"!

(Get it?)

READING AND WRITING

Regardless of our preferred learning styles we all need to develop good reading and writing skills and will rely heavily on these in our learning.

However…

Don't just write. Think first and then write and you will find that you will write just that little bit better. As you are revising: think-communicate-write and you will recall information that little bit better.

To remember spellings for example: write the word correctly, say it out loud, cover it over and now write it again. Check it and if correct move on. If not, repeat the process until you are correct. You will probably find the word and its spelling sticks now. You might do the same with definitions of key words or for words and phrases in a language.

And don't just read. Read-think-communicate. After you have read something then turn the book over and recall the information. Then tell someone-else about it and you are likely to remember it much better.

Try to make difficult things real and personal to you. Imaging you earn £15,000 per year and spend £16,000 on your credit card. Then imagine your credit bill is currently £140,000 and what do you have? Well, add seven zeros to each figure and change the £ to $ and you have the state of the American economy!

USE MY HIERACHY

When you note things and explain things then use Descriptive-Reflective-Speculative. And go for five! (For reasons why five, see Chapter Two.)

Descriptive is "What" or "How"- note 5 things that describe something or 5 steps for doing something (especially useful for mathematical operations). Then note 3 to 5 points that explain it. Perhaps 3 to 5 reasons for and 3 to 5 reasons against something happening. Reflective is "Why"- understand the why and you will recall the what better. Finally draw conclusions... this is the speculative step and further aids the recall of what, how and why.

AND FINALLY

Take a look at my file card system for revision that follows this chapter. You might like to scan the page and print it out on card and actually use it. It's a useful way of interacting with your learning. Transfer key notes, steps, diagrams etc to it as you revise. Keep one file card per topic or sub-topic and on the back write a question to test yourself. You have now a neat way of organising information. When you have covered a number of topics then form your cards into a pack with the question side up and answer the questions in turn. If you can't remember the answer or can't do the sum, for example; then turn your card over and follow the steps.

I also include a list of connectives: learn them and use them when you write in exams, they will help you to express your knowledge more precisely.

Strategies for Outstanding Learning (1):
File Cards for Revision

Picture/Diagram/Example

Subject:

_____

Topic:

_____

Revision Card Number:

Descriptive Box WHAT OR HOW

> 1

> 2

> 3

> 4

> 5

Reflective Box WHY

> 1

> 2

> 3

Speculative Box IF /CONCLUSIONS

Key Words/Phrases Box

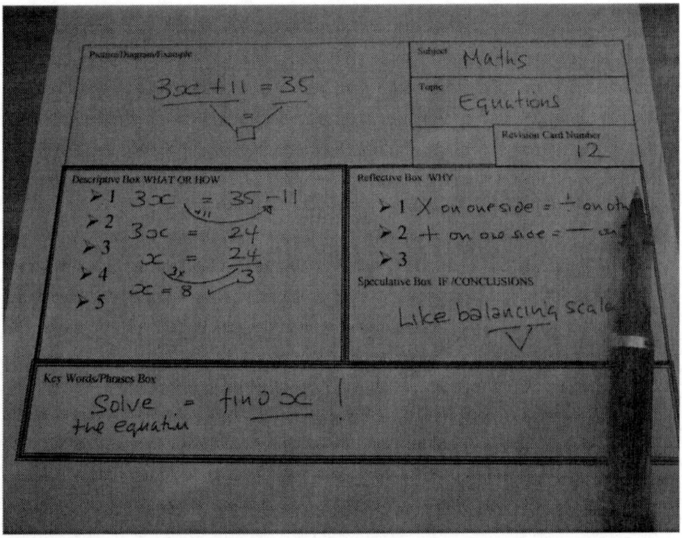
Maths
Equations
Revision Card Number
12
3x + 11 = 35
Descriptive Box WHAT OR HOW
Reflective Box WHY
Speculative Box IF /CONCLUSIONS
Like balancing scale
Key Words/Phrases Box
Solve the equation = find x !

Strategies for Outstanding Learning (2):
Use Descriptive-Reflective-Speculative

FIRST
DESCRIBE THE SCENE
EXPLAIN THE FACTS
EXPLAIN THE SEQUENCE OR STEPS IN DOING SOMETHING

THEN
EXPLAIN THE FEELINGS
EXPLAIN THE CONSEQUENCES
EXPLAIN THE RESULT

FINALLY
DRAW CONCLUSIONS
PRESENT NEW IDEAS
SPECULATE UPON POSSIBILITIES

Think:

How

Why?

If

Strategies for Outstanding Learning (3):
Use connectives, in thinking, speaking and writing

If you wish to illustrate:
compared with
in the same way
equally
similarly
as well as

If you wish to contrast:
however
but
on the one hand, on the other
yet
although

If you wish to persuade:
obviously
of course
clearly
surely
certainly

To give an opinion:
it would seem that
possibly
maybe
perhaps
definitely

To write about cause and effect:
thus
as a result of
so therefore
because
in order to

To extend your writing:
Firstly... Secondly... Thirdly... Next... Finally...

To conclude: *In conclusion, finally, in the end, on the whole, in summary,*

Strategies for Outstanding Learning (4):
Use a consistent approach to studying subjects

(E.g. For thinking about, writing about and comparing poems and prose learn a system and take yourself through it step-by-step. Learn key words to look out for and to discuss...)

P1 DEFINE THE THEME OF THE WRITING
AND KEY WORDS IN EXAM QUESTION

TITLE:
The narrative of....

P2 STRUCTURE

What?   **Why?**

KEY WORDS
RHYME, RHYTHM, NUMBER OF STANZAS, REPETITION, SYMMETRY, PARAGRAPHING, PUNCTUATION, STAND OUTS

P3 LANGUAGE

What?   **Example:**   **Why?**

KEY WORDS FORMAL OR COLLOQUIAL, DIALECT, IMAGES, SIMILES, METAPHORS, ONOMATAPOEIA, ALLITERATION, ASSONANCE, PERSONIFICATION, WHOSE VOICE? TONE OF THE LANGUAGE? ATMOSPHERE CREATED BY LANGUAGE? QUESTIONS? COMANDS!

P4 WRITER'S INTENTIONS, FEELINGS, IDEAS, THOUGHTS, BELIEFS

What?   **Why?**

P5 WHAT I LIKE ABOUT THIS PIECE OF WRITING   WHY?

HOW I RELATE THIS TO MY OWN FEELINGS, VALUES, BELIEFS, THOUGHTS, etc.:

Strategies for Outstanding Learning (5):
Plan using templates

(E.g. For writing persuasively devise a planning template and stick to is when writing; it will help you to organise your thoughts.)

P4 POET'S INTENTIONS, FEELINGS, IDEAS, THOUGHTS, BELIEFS

What?	**Why?**
PLAN FIRST What do I want to persuade about?	What
Reasons why?	Why (Go for Five)
Audience: Formal/Informal style?	To whom Style?
<u>PARAGRAPH 1= SHOCK IMAGE!</u> Imagine..... That's why I am asking you to....	<u>P1= SHOCK IMAGE!</u>
Introduce yourself and your reasons *for writing this*	<u>P 2= GIVE THEM "HEAD" REASONS</u>

<u>PARAGRAPH 2= GIVE THEM "HEAD" REASONS</u>

   Firstly, let me give you the economic reasons. (....costs the nation 70 billion pounds a year...)

   Secondly, when I surveyed my two hundred friends on Facebook about this, 75% agreed we need action. (... I am sure that all of these would...)

   Thirdly, you may have seen this very issue featured recently on the One Show: all the experts agreed with us.

PARAGRAPH 3= APPEAL TO THEM BEING GOOD MEMBERS OF THE COMMUNITY

P3= APPEAL TO THEM BEING GOOD MEMBERS OF THE COMMUNITY

As a caring (person, publication, friend) I am sure you will agree with me when I say that (helping me/ doing this) would be good for us all. It would------------------------,------------ and----------------------!

PARAGRAPH 4= APPEAL TO THEIR HEART

P4= APPEAL TO THEIR HEART

How would you feel if————— —————?

PARAGRAPH 5= COUNTER POSSBLE ARGUMENTS

P5= COUNTER POSSBLE ARGUMENTS

Perhaps you are thinking that you can't do this because (1,2,3) Good points! But consider this:

PARAGRAPH 6= SINGLE SENTENCE PARAGRAPH

P6= SINGLE SENTENCE PARAGRAPH

Think alliteration, think slogan.

PARAGRAPH 7= IN CONCLUSION

P7= IN CONCLUSION

In conclusion….

Don't be a fly on the wall or dead in the ointment! Don't allow *(par 1 to happen)*..

Please, *(do what I ask)!*

Strategies for Outstanding Learning (6):
Use metaphor and simile to stimulate your creative thinking

Oh, if I were writing me

Oh, if I was writing me as an animal; what an animal I would be!
I would, almost certainly, be like a _____.
They are _____, _____ and_____.
They move_____ through the world _____ly,
_____ly,
and _____ly.
Oh, if only I was writing me!

Yet, if I was writing me as a plant; what a plant I would be!
I would, almost certainly, be a_____.
My roots would be strong, true and spread evenly under me.
No wind would _____or_____,
nor_____me.
Oh, if only I was writing me!

If I was writing me what could I, would I, not be able to be?
As a colour I would be_____: _____,_____
and_____ because this colours me.

As a shape, I would be _____
because this surrounds me.
As a a feeling I would _____
because this abounds in me.
As a concept, I would be _____
because this astounds me.

As a song I would be_____
because this gives a quiet and subtle voice to me.

Yet no simile, metaphor or dream truly writes me.

No animal, plant, colour nor shape nor feeling encompasses me.

No concept conceptualises, nor song sings me.

Take me, leave me but let me be
confusingly, wholly, uniquely
just me.

Because it's scary, dark and cold alone in there